T0137279

Cyber Threat Intelligence for the Internet of Things

Elias Bou-Harb • Nataliia Neshenko

Cyber Threat Intelligence for the Internet of Things

 Springer

Elias Bou-Harb
Information Systems and Cyber Security
The University of Texas at San Antonio
San Antonio, TX, USA

Nataliia Neshenko
Computer & Electrical Engineering
Florida Atlantic University
Boca Raton, FL, USA

ISBN 978-3-030-45860-7   ISBN 978-3-030-45858-4   (eBook)
https://doi.org/10.1007/978-3-030-45858-4

This Springer imprint is published by the registered company Springer Nature Switzerland AG
The registered company address is: Gewerbestrasse 11, 6330 Cham, Switzerland

Preface

Advancements in computing, communication, and sensing technologies are making it possible to embed, control, and gather vital information from tiny devices that are being deployed and utilized in practically every aspect of our modernized society. From smart home appliances to municipal water and electric industrial facilities to our everyday work environments, the next Internet frontier dubbed as the Internet of Things (IoT) is promising to revolutionize our lives and tackle some of our nation's most pressing challenges. While the seamless interconnection of IoT devices with the physical realm is envisioned to bring a plethora of critical improvements on many aspects and in diverse domains, it will undoubtedly pave the way for attackers that will target and exploit such devices, threatening the integrity of their data and the reliability of critical infrastructure. Furthermore, such compromised devices will undeniably be leveraged as the next generation of botnets, given their increased processing capabilities and abundant bandwidth. The aim of this book is to generate cyber threat intelligence related to Internet-scale inference and evaluation of malicious activities generated by compromised IoT devices to facilitate prompt detection, mitigation, and prevention of IoT exploitation.

In this context, the book initially provides a comprehensive classification of state-of-the-art surveys, which address various dimensions of the IoT paradigm. This aims at facilitating IoT research endeavors by amalgamating, comparing, and contrasting dispersed research contributions. Subsequently, it provides a unique taxonomy, which sheds the light on IoT vulnerabilities, their attack vectors, impacts on numerous security objectives, attacks which exploit such vulnerabilities, corresponding remediation methodologies, and currently offered operational cybersecurity capabilities to infer and monitor such weaknesses. This aims at providing the reader with a multidimensional research perspective related to IoT vulnerabilities, including their technical details and consequences, which is postulated to be leveraged for remediation objectives. While several demonstrations exist in the literature describing the exploitation procedures of a number of IoT devices, the real time inference, characterization, and analysis of unsolicited IoT devices that are currently deployed in the wild are still in their infancy. The book addresses this imperative task by leveraging active and passive measurements to report on unsolicited Internet-scale

IoT devices. This work renders a first step towards exploring the utilization of passive measurements in combination with the results of active measurements to shed the light on the Internet-scale insecurities of the IoT paradigm. By correlating results of Internet-wide scanning with Internet background radiation traffic, this work discloses numerous compromised IoT devices in diverse sectors, including critical infrastructure and smart home appliances. To this end, it also analyzes their generated traffic to create effective mitigation signatures that could be deployed at local IoT realms. To support large-scale empirical data analytics in the context of IoT, the inferred and extracted IoT malicious raw data through an authenticated platform is made available. The outcomes of this work confirm the existence of such compromised devices on an Internet scale, while the generated inferences and insights are postulated to be employed for inferring other similarly compromised IoT devices, in addition to contributing to IoT cybersecurity situational awareness.

San Antonio, TX, USA   Elias Bou-Harb
Boca Raton, FL, USA   Nataliia Neshenko
January 2020

Acknowledgements

This work was supported by a grant from the U.S. National Science Foundation (NSF) (Office of Advanced Cyberinfrastructure (OAC) #1953050).

Contents

Chapter 1
Introduction

The conception of the prominent Internet-of-Things (IoT) notion is envisioned to improve the quality of modern life. People-centric IoT solutions, for instance, significantly enhance daily routines of elderly and disabled people, thus increasing their autonomy and self-confidence [8]. Implantable and wearable IoT devices monitor and extract vital measurements to enable the real-time emergency alerting in order to increase patients' chances of survival [5]. This emerging technology is also being leveraged to reduce response times in reacting to abrupt health incidents such as the sudden infant death syndrome during sleep [9]. Moreover, advanced solutions for in-home rehabilitation strive to revolutionize physical therapy [3], while the Autism Glass [18] aims at aiding autistic children to recognize emotions of other people in real-time [16].

Safety-centric IoT solutions endeavor to minimize hazardous scenarios and situations. For example, the concept of connected vehicles prevents the driver from deviating from proper trajectory paths or bumping into objects. Further, such concept enables the automatic emergency notification of nearest road and medical assistance in case of accidents [6]. Additionally, autonomous, self-driving mining equipment keeps workers away from unsafe areas, while location and proximity IoT sensors allow miners to avoid dangerous situations [7]. Moreover, deployed IoT sensors at factories monitor environmental pollution and chemical leaks in water supply, while smoke, toxic gases and temperature sensors coupled with warning systems prevent ecological disasters [14]. Indeed, a number of case-studies report on the significant impact of IoT on natural resources' integrity and consumption. For instance, water pressure sensors in pipelines monitor flow activity and notify operators in case of a leak, while smart IoT devices and systems enable citizens to control water and energy consumption [14]. In fact, the IoT notion is introducing notable solutions for contemporary operations, well-being and safety. In this context, several ongoing IoT endeavors, such as those illustrated in Fig. 1.1, promise to transform modern life and business models, hence improving efficiency, service level, and customer satisfaction.

© Springer Nature Switzerland AG 2020
E. Bou-Harb, N. Neshenko, *Cyber Threat Intelligence for the Internet of Things*,
https://doi.org/10.1007/978-3-030-45858-4_1

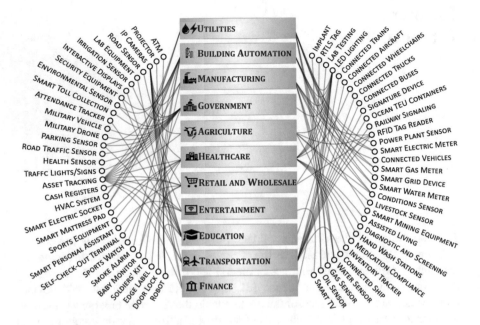

Fig. 1.1 IoT's penetration into contemporary life

1.1 Context and Motivation

Undeniable benefits proposed by the IoT paradigm, nevertheless, are coupled with serious security flaws. Profit-driven businesses and time-to-market along with the shortage of related legislation have stimulated manufacturers to overlook security considerations and to design potentially vulnerable IoT devices, opening the door for adversaries, which often exploit such devices with little or no effort. The negligence of a number of security considerations enables the exposure of sensitive information ranging from unprotected video streaming of baby monitors [19] to the uploading of unauthorized voice recordings, emails and passwords by Internet-connected IoT toys [11]. Moreover, poorly designed devices allow the execution of arbitrary commands and re-programming of device firmware [2]. Indeed, given the Internet-wide deployment of IoT devices, such malicious manipulations generate a profound impact on the security and the resiliency of the entire Internet. Among the many cases that recently attracted the public attention, the cyber attack launched by the IoT-specific malware Mirai [13] provides a clear example of the severity of the threat caused by instrumenting exploited IoT devices. In this case, the primary DNS provider in the US, Dyn, became the target of an orchestrated Denial of Service (DoS) attack, jeopardizing the profit and reputation of its clients. In fact, Dyn lost nearly 8% of its customers right after the mentioned attack [1]. Such and other security incidents impair the confidence in the IoT paradigm, hindering its widespread implementation in consumer markets and critical infrastructure. While the disclosure of private and confidential information coupled with the launch of debilitating DoS attacks cause various privacy violations and business disruptions, the most significant danger from exposed IoT devices remains the threat to people's lives and well-being. Security risks rendered by unauthorized access and reconfiguration of IoT medical devices, including implantable cardiac devices, have been already confirmed by the Food and Drug Administration (FDA) [10]. Moreover, the hacking of traffic lights [17] and connected vehicles [12, 15] not only causes havoc and increases pollution, but also possesses the capability to cause injury and drastic accidents leading to fatalities. While benefits from using these IoT devices and corresponding technologies possibly outweigh the risks, undoubtedly, IoT security at large should be carefully and promptly addressed.

Several technical difficulties, including limited storage, power, and computational capabilities, challenge addressing various IoT security requirements. For instance, the simple issue of unauthorized access to IoT devices by applying default user credentials remains largely unsolved. IoT manufacturers, even though aware of this flaw, do not mitigate this risk by design, making consumers take responsibility of this technical task and to update their device firmware. Ironically, close to 48% of consumer individuals are unaware that their connected devices could be used to conduct a cyber attack, and around 40% of those individuals never perform firmware updates, while arguing that it is the responsibility of device manufacturers or software developers to remediate this security risk [4].

1.2 Objectives and Contributions

The aim of this book is to generate cyber threat intelligence related to Internet-scale inference and evaluation of malicious activities generated by compromised IoT devices to facilitate prompt detection, mitigation and prevention of IoT exploitations.

In this context, we frame our objectives in the following:

- To employ an exhaustive, multidimensional approach, which specifically addresses the topic of IoT vulnerabilities. More imperatively, we attempt to (1) comprehend the impact of such ever-evolving vulnerabilities on various security objectives, (2) identify the vectors which permit the rise of these vulnerabilities in the first place, (3) characterize and analyze methods, techniques and approaches, which can be leveraged by an attacker to exploit such vulnerabilities, (4) explore and assess possible remediation strategies, which aim at mitigating the identified vulnerabilities, and (5) shed the light on currently offered IoT cyber security situational awareness capabilities, which endeavor to identify, attribute, characterize and respond to such vulnerabilities or their possible exploitation attempts.

- To propose an approach that can practically identify Internet-wide compromised IoT devices, in near real-time.
- To generate relevant intelligence regarding large-scale IoT exploitation to derive situational awareness.

We achieved our goal by analyzing the aforementioned dimensions as they inter-relay with certain identified IoT vulnerabilities, and by a thorough investigation of a significant amount of network telescope data and correlation the digital information with the physical presence of unsolicited IoT devices in the attempt to profile IoT exploitations. Precisely, we frame the contributions of this work as follows:

- Amalgamating and classifying currently available IoT-relevant literature surveys to highlight research trends in this emerging field and to facilitate research initiation by new researchers through eliminating repetitive research efforts.
- Introducing a unique taxonomy by emphasizing and discussing IoT vulnera-bilities in the context of various, previously unanalyzed dimensions through comparing, contrasting and analyzing near 100 research contributions. This aims at putting forward a new perspective related to IoT security, which we hope could be leveraged by readers from various backgrounds to address the issue of IoT security from their respective aspects of interest.
- Laying down a set of inferences, insights, challenges and open issues in the context of the discussed taxonomy and findings. Such outcomes facilitate future research endeavors in this imperative IoT security area.
- Proposing and evaluating an innovative approach to infer, characterize and attribute unsolicited Internet-scale IoT devices by correlating passive and the results of active empirical measurements. To the best of our knowledge, this work is among the first to explore such approach, which addresses the IoT paradigm.
- Generating IoT-specific malicious signatures by scrutinizing passive measure-ments. Such signatures, which are based on fuzzy hashes, are envisioned to be employed for deployments in local IoT realms for effective mitigation as well as to infer other Internet-wide unsolicited IoT devices. As noted in [20], IoT-specific empirical attack signatures currently do not exist, rendering the proposed approach highly impactful and operationally very beneficial.
- Reporting the alarming number of compromised IoT devices related to smart home appliances, critical infrastructure, and automated control sectors. In this context, we generate amalgamated statistics related to these inferred and exploited IoT devices, including, their hosting environments.
- Implementing a web-based platform, which is capable of aggregating data from multiple sources and promptly generating relevant intelligence, while requiring minimal human interaction. We also make publicly accessible all the generated inferences, including, IoT malicious raw data. We postulate that such generated cyber threat intelligence could be exploited, in near real-time, for effective IoT cyber security situational awareness, notification, and remediation.

Overall, by leveraging empirical measurements we explore and investigate meth-ods and techniques to infer unsolicited IoT devices, capture notions of maliciousness related to those unsolicited devices and to enhance practices. The operational outcome includes a web-based platform for accessing IoT malicious empirical data which can be extracted from darknet data and shared at large with the research community to facilitate forensic investigations of IoT-relevant data.

1.3 Notes on This Book's Organization

The book comprises of following five chapters. In Chap. 2, we provide a taxonomy which emphasizes IoT vulnerabilities and elaborates on literature approaches, which address their various dimensions. In Chap. 3, we detail and evaluate the proposed approach for inferring IoT exploitation and describe its aims, employed methods, and techniques. In this context, we elaborate on the produced insights and inferences. In Chap. 4 we detail design and implementation of an automated platform for generating intelligence regarding large-scale IoT exploitation. In Chap. 5, we conclude this book and pinpoint several research challenges and topics that aim at paving the way for future work in the area of IoT security.

References

1. Weagle, Stephanie. Financial impact of Mirai DDoS attack on Dyn revealed in new data. [Online]. Available: https://www.corero.com/blog/797-financial-impact-of-mirai-ddos-attack-on-dyn-revealed-in-new-data.html. Accessed 2018-03-05.
2. Elisa Bertino and Nayeem Islam. Botnets and internet of things security. *Computer*, 50(2):76–79, 2017.
3. Igor Bisio, Alessandro Delfino, Fabio Lavagetto, and Andrea Sciarrone. Enabling IoT for in-home rehabilitation: Accelerometer signals classification methods for activity and movement recognition. *IEEE Internet of Things Journal*, 4(1):135–146, 2017.
4. Canonical Ltd. Who should bear the cost of iot security: consumers or vendors? [Online]. Available: https://insights.ubuntu.com/2017/02/07/who-should-bear-the-cost-of-iot-security-consumers-or-vendors/. Accessed 2018-03-05.
5. Marie Chan, Daniel Estève, Jean-Yves Fourniols, Christophe Escriba, and Eric Campo. Smart wearable systems: Current status and future challenges. *Artificial intelligence in medicine*, 56(3):137–156, 2012.
6. Riccardo Coppola and Maurizio Morisio. Connected car: technologies, issues, future trends. *ACM Computing Surveys (CSUR)*, 49(3):46, 2016.
7. Centric Digital. Internet of things applications part 2: The mining industry. [Online]. Available: https://centricdigital.com/blog/digital-trends/internet-of-things-applications-pt2-the-mining-industry/. Accessed 2018-03-05.
8. Mari Carmen Domingo. An overview of the internet of things for people with disabilities. *Journal of Network and Computer Applications*, 35(2):584–596, 2012.
9. André G Ferreira, Duarte Fernandes, Sérgio Branco, João L Monteiro, Jorge Cabral, André P Catarino, and Ana M Rocha. A smart wearable system for sudden infant death syndrome monitoring. In *Industrial Technology (ICIT), 2016 IEEE International Conference on*, pages 1920–1925. IEEE, 2016.

10. U.S. Food and Drug Administration. Cybersecurity vulnerabilities identified in St. Jude medical's implantable cardiac devices and merlin@home transmitter: FDA safety communication. [Online]. Available: https://www.fda.gov/MedicalDevices/Safety/AlertsandNotices/ucm535843.htm. Accessed 2018-03-05.

11. Franceschi-Bicchierai, Lorenzo. How this internet of things stuffed animal can be remotely turned into a spy device. [Online]. Available: https://motherboard.vice.com/en_us/article/qkm48b/how-this-internet-of-things-teddy-bear-can-be-remotely-turned-into-a-spy-device. Accessed 2018-03-05.

12. The Guardian. Team of hackers take remote control of tesla models from 12 miles away. [Online]. Available: https://www.theguardian.com/technology/2016/sep/20/tesla-model-s-chinese-hack-remote-control-brakes. Accessed 2018-03-05.

13. Ben Herzberg, Dima Bekerman, and Igal Zifman. Breaking down mirai: An iot ddos botnet analysis. [Online]. Available: https://www.incapsula.com/blog/malware-analysis-mirai-ddos-botnet.html. Accessed 2018-03-05.

14. In association with the Korea Research Institute for Human Settlements (KRIHS) Inter-American Development Bank (IDB). Smart cities - international case studies. [Online]. Available: http://www.iadb.org/en/topics/emerging-and-sustainable-cities/international-case-studies-of-smart-cities.20271.html. Accessed 2018-03-05.

15. Cara McGoogan. BMW, Audi and Toyota cars can be unlocked and started with hacked radios. [Online]. Available: http://www.telegraph.co.uk/technology/2016/03/23/hackers-can-unlock-and-start-dozens-of-high-end-cars-through-the/. Accessed 2018-03-05.

16. Patel, Prachi. Autism glass takes top student health tech prize. [Online]. Available: https://www.scientificamerican.com/article/autism-glass-takes-top-student-health-tech-prize-slide-show1/. Accessed 2018-03-05.

17. Mark Prigg. How to get green lights all the way to work: Hackers reveal how simple it is to control traffic lights in major cities using just a laptop. [Online]. Available: http://www.dailymail.co.uk/sciencetech/article-2730096/How-green-lights-way-work-Hackers-reveal-simple-control-traffic-lights-major-cities-using-just-laptop.html. Accessed 2018-03-05.

18. Stanford University. The autism glass project at Stanford medicine. [Online]. Available: http://autismglass.stanford.edu/. Accessed 2018-03-05.

19. Mark Stanislav and Tod Beardsley. Hacking iot: A case study on baby monitor exposures and vulnerabilities. *Rapid 7*, 2015. [Online]. Available: https://www.rapid7.com/docs/Hacking-IoT-A-Case-Study-on-Baby-Monitor-Exposures-and-Vulnerabilities.pdf. Accessed 2018-03-05.

20. Tianlong Yu, Vyas Sekar, Srinivasan Seshan, Yuvraj Agarwal, and Chenren Xu. Handling a trillion (unfixable) flaws on a billion devices: Rethinking network security for the internet-of-things. In *Proceedings of the 14th ACM Workshop on Hot Topics in Networks*, page 5. ACM, 2015.

Chapter 2
Taxonomy of IoT Vulnerabilities

Although a plethora of security mechanisms currently exist aiming at enhancing IoT security, many research and operational problems remain unsolved, raising various concerns and thus undermining the confidence in the IoT paradigm. By thoroughly exploring the IoT security literature, one can identify several addressed topics related to IoT security. These include IoT-specific security mechanisms related to intrusion detection and threat modeling, as well as broader related topics in the context of emerging IoT protocols and technologies, to name a few. To this end, we perceive a lack of an exhaustive, multidimensional approach, which specifically addresses the topic of IoT vulnerabilities. More imperatively, we pinpoint the scarcity of research works, which attempt to (1) comprehend the impact of such ever-evolving vulnerabilities on various security objectives, (2) identify the vectors which permit the rise of these vulnerabilities in the first place, (3) characterize and analyze methods, techniques and approaches, which can be leveraged by an attacker to exploit such vulnerabilities, (4) explore and assess possible remediation strategies, which aim at mitigating the identified vulnerabilities, and (5) shed the light on currently offered IoT cyber security situational awareness capabilities, which endeavor to identify, attribute, characterize and respond to such vulnerabilities or their possible exploitation attempts.

To this end, in this chapter, we uniquely approach IoT security by analyzing the aforementioned dimensions as they inter-relay with certain identified IoT vulnerabilities. In the next section, we review and classify related surveys on various IoT-relevant topics and demonstrate the added value of the offered work. In Sect. 2.2, we describe the survey's methodology, leading to the taxonomy. In

---

This chapter was partially adopted from Nataliia Neshenko, Elias Bou-Harb, Jorge Crichigno, Georges Kaddoum, and Nasir Ghani. Demystifying IoT Security: an Exhaustive Survey on IoT Vulnerabilities and a First Empirical Look on Internet-scale IoT Exploitations. *IEEE Communications Surveys & Tutorials*, 2019.

Sect. 2.3, we pinpoint the identified and extracted vulnerabilities, which form the basis of the taxonomy. In Sect. 2.4, we present the proposed taxonomy, which emphasizes IoT vulnerabilities and elaborates on literature approaches, which address their various dimensions.

2.1   Research Trends in the Field

The rapid growth and adoption of the IoT paradigm have induced an enormous attention from the research community. To highlight the latest findings and research directions in such an evolving field, a plethora of surveys were put forward to shed the light on recent IoT trends and challenges such as enabling technologies, application domains, and security methodologies. In this section, we scrutinize and classify a significantly representative number of such related surveys to outline their contributions in addition to clarifying how the presented work advances the state-of-the-art.

Atzori et al. [9] discussed two different perspectives of IoT research, namely, Internet-oriented or Things-oriented. The authors reviewed application domains, research challenges, and the most relevant enabling technologies with a focus on their role rather than their technical details. The authors further discussed the importance of security and indicated that numerous constraints such as limited energy and computation power of the IoT devices hinder the implementation of complex (and perhaps effective) security mechanisms.

In an alternate work, Gubbi et al. [61] elaborated on IoT-centric application domains and their corresponding challenges. The authors reviewed international activities in the field and presented a cloud-focused vision for the implementation of the IoT. The authors advocated that the application development platform dubbed as Aneka [149] allows the necessary flexibility to address the needs of different IoT sensors. The authors also pinpointed the importance of security in the cloud to fully realize the contemporary vision of the IoT paradigm.

Further, Xu et al. [33] presented an analysis of the core IoT enabling technologies and multi-layer architectures, along with an overview of industrial applications in the IoT context. The authors indicated that due to specific characteristics of IoT such as deployment, mobility and complexity, such paradigm suffers from severe security weaknesses, which cannot be tolerated in the realm of an industrial IoT.

Additionally, Al-Fuqaha et al. [3] reviewed IoT application domains, enabling technologies, their roles and the functionality of communication protocols adopted by the IoT. The authors distinguished between six core components that are crucial to delivering IoT services. These include identification, sensing, communication, computation, services, and semantics. The latter dimensions are presented in conjunction with their related standards, technologies and implementations. The authors analyzed numerous challenges and issues, including, security, privacy, performance, reliability, and management. To this end, they argued that the lack of common standards among IoT architectures render a core challenge hindering the protection of IoT from debilitating cyber threats.

A more recent study in the context of IoT is presented by Atzori et al. [10]. The authors synthesized the evolution of IoT and distinguished its three generations. According to the authors, these three epochs are respectively labeled as (1) tagged things, (2) a web of things, and (3) social IoT, cloud computing, and semantic data. The authors further debated that current technological advances on many aspects would indeed facilitate the realization of the next generation of IoT. By reviewing technologies attributed to each period, the authors presented certain desired transformational characteristics and applications.

Alternatively, Perera et al. [102] approached the IoT from a context-aware perspective. Aiming to identify available context-aware techniques and to analyze their applicability, the authors surveyed 50 diverse projects in this field and proposed a taxonomy of future models, techniques, functionality, and strategies. The authors noted that although security and privacy are addressed in the application layer, nevertheless, there still exists a need to pay close attention to such requirement in the middleware layer. The authors also shed the light on the security and privacy functionalities related to the surveyed projects.

While the aforementioned noteworthy research contributions specifically addressed the topics of IoT architectures and corresponding technologies, a number of other studies delved deep into its security aspects.

For instance, Sicari et al. [130] centered their work on the analysis of available solutions in the field of IoT security. Since IoT communication protocols and technologies differ from traditional IT realms, their security solutions ought to be different as well. The survey of a broad number of academic works led to the conclusion that despite numerous attempts in this field, many challenges and research questions remain open. In particular, the authors stressed the fact that a systematic and a unified vision to guarantee IoT security is still lacking. The authors also provided analysis of international projects in the field and noted that such endeavors are typically aimed at designing and implementing IoT-specific applications.

Further, Nia et al. [91] used Cisco seven-level reference model [22] to present various corresponding attack scenarios. The authors explored numerous IoT targeted attacks and pinpointed their possible mitigation approaches. The authors highlighted the importance of possessing a proactive approach for securing the IoT environment.

In contrast, Granjal et al. [59] analyzed how existing security mechanisms satisfy a number of IoT requirements and objectives. The authors centered their discussion around the IPv6 over Low-Power Wireless Personal Area Networks (6LoWPAN) concept [126], transportation, routing, and application layers. Among other limitations, they identified several constraints of key management mechanisms.

Very recently, Ouaddah et al. [94] presented a quantitative and a qualitative evaluation of available access control solutions for IoT. The authors highlighted how each solution achieved various security requirements, noting that the adoption of traditional approaches cannot be applied directly to IoT in many cases. The authors also declared that centralized and distributed approaches could complement each other when designing IoT-tailored access control.

Additionally, Roman et al. [116] centered their survey on numerous security features in addition to elaborating on the challenges of a distributed architecture to understand its viability for IoT. The authors concluded that while a distributed architecture might reduce the impact caused by a successful attack, it might also augment the number of attack vectors.

Alternatively, Weber and Studer in [147] discussed numerous IoT security threats and presented a review of available legal frameworks. The authors indicated that, based on available studies, the most significant progress in this area had been made within the European Union. Nevertheless, the authors revealed that IoT practical applications are still at their infancy.

Moreover, Zhang et al. [158] approached IoT security by analyzing reports related to IoT incidents. To this end, data mining techniques were leveraged to design a capability which crawled Internet publications, including academic research, news, blogs, and cyber reports. By correlating real IoT incidents with the available security solutions, the authors unveiled five weak areas in the context of IoT security, which require prompt attention. These areas include LAN and environmental mistrust, over-privileged applications, insufficient authentication and implementation flaws. The authors identified several domains that would require further exploration in order to advance the area of IoT security. The entire collection of accumulated and generated data and statistics are made available online by the authors.

In an alternative work, Alaba et al. [4] analyzed IoT security by reviewing existing security solutions and proposing a taxonomy of current threats and vulnerabilities in the context of various IoT deployment environments. Particularly, the taxonomy distinguished between four classes, including, application, architecture, communication, and data. The authors examined various threats and discussed them for each deployment domain. Moreover, a number of IoT challenges, which currently face the research community, were discussed. In this context, the authors argued that the heterogeneity of IoT devices along with their resource limitations define a serious issue, which hinders the scalability of possible security solutions.

In addition, Gendreau and Moorman [55] reviewed intrusion detection techniques proposed for the IoT. The survey validates the assertion that the concept of intrusion detection in the context of IoT remains at its infancy, despite numerous attempts. The authors also indicated that prevention of unauthorized access is a challenging goal due to the limited computational power of the IoT devices.

Zarpelão et al. [156] reached the same conclusion. The authors surveyed intrusion detection research efforts for IoT and classified them based on detection method, placement strategy, security threat, and validation strategy. The main observation of the authors is that intrusion detection schemes for IoT are still emerging. In particular, they noted that the proposed solutions do not cover a broad range of attacks and IoT technologies. Moreover, many of the currently offered schemes have never been thoroughly evaluated and validated.

To clarify the aforementioned works, we now present Table 2.1, which summaries and classifies the contributions of the reviewed surveys. This aims at permitting readers from diverse backgrounds and new researchers in the IoT field to

Table 2.1 A classification of reviewed surveys on IoT

Author	Protocols and technologies	Application domains	Context awareness	Legal frameworks	Attacks	Access models	Security protocols	Intrusion detection techniques
Atzori et al. [10]	✓	✓						
Gubbi et al. [60]	✓	✓						
Xu et al. [33]	✓	✓						
Al-Fuqaha et al. [3]	✓	✓						
Atzori et al. [10]	✓	✓						
Perera et al. [101]			✓					
Sicari et al. [129]						✓	✓	
Nia et al. [90]	✓				✓		✓	
Granjal et al. [58]	✓					✓	✓	
Ouaddah et al. [93]	✓					✓		
Roman et al. [115]					✓	✓	✓	
Weber and Studer [146]				✓				
Zhang et al. [157]					✓	✓		✓
Alaba et al. [4]	✓	✓			✓	✓	✓	
Gendreau and Moorman [54]								✓
Zarpelão et al. [155]								✓

quickly and easily pinpoint already available contributions dealing with a common set of topics. It is evident that such efforts offer detailed studies related to IoT architectures and protocols, enabling technologies, threat modeling and remediation mechanisms. From such works, we noticed the lack of surveys, which specifically focus on the notion of IoT vulnerabilities. Particularly, we identify the research gap rendered by the nonexistence of a multidimensional perspective related to such vulnerabilities; dealing with the comprehension of their impact on different security objectives, identification of ways attackers can exploit them to threaten the IoT paradigm and the resiliency of the entire Internet, elaboration of their corresponding remediation strategies and currently available cyber security awareness capabilities to monitor and infer such "in the wild" exploitations. Motivated by this, we offer such unique taxonomy in this work, which aims at shedding the light on IoT vulnerabilities and literature approaches which address their impact, consequences and operational capabilities. Further, stimulated by the lack of IoT-relevant empirical data and IoT-centric attack signatures [154], this work also alarms about the severity of the IoT paradigm by scrutinizing Internet-scale unsolicited data. To this end, the presented work offers a first-of-a-kind cyber-infrastructure, which aims at sharing the extracted cyber threat information and IoT-tailored empirical data with the research community at large.

2.2 Research Methodology

In this section, we briefly describe the employed systematic methodology, which was adopted to generate the offered taxonomy. The results of this literature survey represent derived findings by thoroughly exploring nearly 100 IoT-specific research works extending from 2005 up to 2017, inclusively; the distribution of which is summarized in Fig. 2.1. Please note that, for completeness purposes, Sect. 5.1 will highlight on few emerging IoT security contributions which have appeared in 2018.

Initially, we meticulously investigated research contributions, which addressed various security aspects of the IoT paradigm. The aim was to extract relevant, common and impactful IoT vulnerabilities. We further confirmed their consistency with several public listings such as [106] and [2]. Subsequently, we attempted to categorize such vulnerabilities by the means they manifest; whether they are specifically related to IoT devices, affected by weaknesses in the networking subsystem (i.e., technologies, protocols, etc.) or they are caused by software/application issues. Moreover, we intended to establish a relationship between the inferred and extracted vulnerabilities and the core security objectives (i.e., confidentiality, integrity, availability) that they affect. We were further interested to synthesis how malicious actors would exploit such vulnerabilities. In this context, we selected research contributions in which the authors defined, analyzed, emulated or simulated an attack on the IoT. To identify possible and corresponding remediation techniques

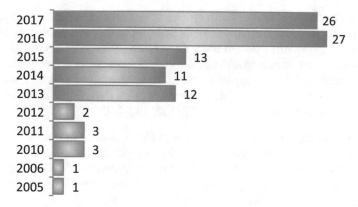

Fig. 2.1 Distribution of analyzed IoT research works by year

for each vulnerability, we extracted specific research works that proposed tailored solutions to address various aspects of IoT security. We categorized such approaches into several common classes. Finally, we intended to shed the light on methods, techniques and cyber security capabilities that would allow the proactive inference, characterization and attribution of malicious activities and emerging vulnerabilities, which might threaten the IoT paradigm. To this end, we explored research works which offered various mechanisms to (1) assess IoT devices and realms in order to discover their inherit or compound vulnerabilities, (2) monitor IoT-generated malicious activities, (3) infer Internet-scale IoT devices as deployed in consumer and Cyber-Physical Systems (CPS) sectors, and (4) identify attacks against IoT environments. Typical search engines and databases such as Google scholar, Scopus and Web of Science were employed to browse and identify relevant literature. IEEE Xplore and ACM digital libraries were the most explored indexing services to accomplish the literature search.

2.3   IoT Vulnerabilities

Based on the previously outlined methodology, an exhaustive analysis of the research works related to the field of IoT security yielded nine (9) classes of IoT vulnerabilities. In this section, we describe such vulnerabilities, which aim at paving the way the elaboration of their multidimensional taxonomy as thoroughly described in Sect. 2.4. For each class of vulnerabilities, we pinpoint a number of representative research works in their corresponding contexts. Please note that these works have been selected based upon their recency and/or significant number of citations. This aims at directing the reader, at an early stage of the book, to relevant works related to the extracted vulnerabilities, noting that Sect. 2.4 will provide an exhaustive review addressing such vulnerabilities and their various dimensions.

Deficient Physical Security The majority of IoT devices operate autonomously in unattended environments [83]. With little effort, an adversary might obtain unauthorized physical access to such devices and thus take control over them. Consequently, an attacker would cause physical damage to the devices, possibly unveiling employed cryptographic schemes, replicating their firmware using malicious node, or simply corrupting their control or cyber data. Representative research contributions in this context include [107, 122, 132, 139, 150, 159].

Insufficient Energy Harvesting IoT devices characteristically have limited energy and do not necessary possess the technology or mechanisms to renew it automatically. An attacker might drain the stored energy by generating flood of legitimate or corrupted messages, rendering the devices unavailable for valid processes or users. A few research works in this area include [24, 100, 138, 142].

Inadequate Authentication The unique constraints within the context of the IoT paradigm such as limited energy and computational power challenge the implementation of complex authentication mechanisms. To this end, an attacker might exploit ineffective authentication approaches to append spoofed malicious nodes or violate data integrity, thus intruding on IoT devices and network communications. Under such circumstances, the exchanged and employed authentication keys are also always at risk of being lost, destroyed, or corrupted. In such cases, when the keys are not being stored or transmitted securely, sophisticated (or otherwise effective) authentication algorithms become insufficient. Research contributions discussing such vulnerability include [50, 63, 73, 90, 105, 143].

Improper Encryption Data protection is of paramount importance in IoT realms, especially those operating in critical CPS (i.e., power utilities, manufacturing plants, building automation, etc.). It is known that encryption is an effective mechanism to store and transmit data in a way that only authorized users can utilize it. As the strength of cryptosystems depend on their designed algorithms, resource limitations of the IoT affects the robustness, efficiency and efficacy of such algorithms. To this end, an attacker might be able to circumvent the deployed encryption techniques to reveal sensitive information or control operations with limited, feasible effort. Representative research contributions in this context include [15, 117, 119, 125, 129, 148].

Unnecessarily Open Ports Various IoT devices have unnecessarily open ports while running vulnerable services, permitting an attacker to connect and exploit a plethora of vulnerabilities. Research works detailing such weaknesses include [6] and [119].

Insufficient Access Control Strong credential management ought to protect IoT devices and data from unauthorized access. It is known that the majority of IoT devices in conjunction with their cloud management solutions do not force a password of sufficient complexity [41]. Moreover, after installation, numerous devices do not request to change the default user credentials. Further, most of the users have elevated permissions. Hence, an adversary could gain unauthorized access to the device, threaten data and the entire Internet. A number of research works dealing with this vulnerability include [6, 129], and [34, 69, 84, 109, 135].

Improper Patch Management Capabilities IoT operating systems and embedded firmware/software should be patched appropriately to continuously minimize attack vectors and augment their functional capabilities. Nevertheless, abundant cases report that many manufacturers either do not recurrently maintain security patches or do not have in place automated patch-update mechanisms. Moreover, even available update mechanisms lack integrity guarantees, rendering them susceptible to being maliciously modified and applied at large. Literature works such as [135], and [13, 14, 28, 72] deal with this identified vulnerability.

Weak Programming Practices Although strong programming practices and injecting security components might increase the resiliency of the IoT, many researchers have reported that countless firmware are released with known vulnerabilities such as backdoors, root users as prime access points, and the lack of Secure Socket Layer (SSL) usage. Hence, an adversary might easily exploit known security weaknesses to cause buffer overflows, information modifications, or gain unauthorized access to the device. Related research contributions include [28, 50, 135], and [25, 40, 45].

Insufficient Audit Mechanism A plethora of IoT devices lack thorough logging procedures, rendering it possible to conceal IoT-generated malicious activities. Research works related to this area include [65, 139], and [151].

2.4 Taxonomy Overview

Figure 2.2 illustrates the structure of the proposed taxonomy. The taxonomy frames and perceives IoT vulnerabilities within the scope of (1) Layers, (2) Security impact, (3) Attacks, (4) Remediation methods, and (5) Situation awareness capabilities. In the sequel, we elaborate on such classes and their rationale.

Layers examines the influence of the components of the IoT realm on IoT vulnerabilities. This class is intuitively divided into three subclasses, namely, Device-based, Network-Based, and Software-based. Device-based addresses those vulnerabilities associated with the hardware elements of the IoT. In contrast, Network-based deals with IoT vulnerabilities caused by weaknesses originating from communication protocols, while Software-based consists of those vulnerabilities related to the firmware and/or the software of IoT devices.

Security Impact evaluates the vulnerabilities based on the threats they pose on core security objectives, known as the CIA triad. Hence, this class deals with Confidentiality, Integrity, and Availability. IoT vulnerabilities which enable unauthorized access to IoT resources and data would be related to Confidentiality. Integrity issues consist of vulnerabilities which allow unauthorized modifications of IoT data and

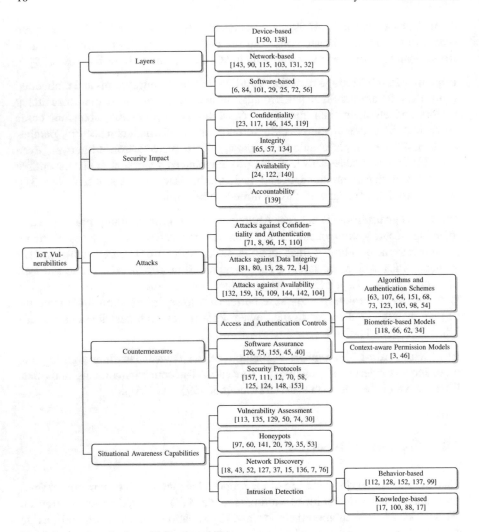

Fig. 2.2 A categorization of IoT vulnerabilities

settings to go undetected. Vulnerabilities which hinder the continuous access to IoT would be related to Availability. It is clear that, given the cross-dependencies among the various security requirements, each identified IoT vulnerability might affect more than one security objective.

Attacks describe the security flaws categorized by the approach in which the inferred IoT vulnerabilities could be exploited. This class is divided into three subclasses, which elaborate on attacks against Confidentiality and Authentication, Data Integrity, and Availability.

Remediation is a classification of the available remediation techniques to mitigate the identified IoT vulnerabilities. This class is divided into Access and

Authentication Controls, Software Assurance, and Security Protocols. Access and Authentication Controls discuss firewalls, algorithms and authentication schemes, biometric-based models, and context-aware permissions. Further, Software Assurance elaborates on the available capabilities to assert integrity constraints, while Security protocols deals with lightweight security schemes for proper remediation.

Last but not least, **Situation Awareness Capabilities** categorizes available techniques for capturing accurate and sufficient information regarding generated malicious activities in the context of the IoT. This class elaborates on Vulnerability Assessment, Honeypots, Network Discovery, and Intrusion Detection. Vulnerability assessment deals with methods and techniques, which the research and cyber security operation communities can employ to assess IoT devices and their vulnerabilities (including 0-day vulnerabilities). Such approaches might include testbeds, attack simulation methods, and fuzzing techniques. Additionally, honeypots provide capabilities, which aim at capturing IoT-specific malicious activities for further investigation, while network discovery addresses methods for Internet-scale identification of vulnerable and compromised IoT devices. Finally, intrusion detection would detail detection methods applicable for inferring and characterizing IoT-centric malicious activities. We now elaborate on the details of the aforementioned dimensions.

2.5 Layers

Broadly, IoT architectures and paradigms consist of three layers, namely, devices, network subsystems, and applications. IoT devices are typically responsible for sensing their environment by capturing cyber-physical data, while communication protocols handle two-way data transmission to the application layer, which in turns generates analytics and instruments the user interface. Indeed, security vulnerabilities exist at each tier of such an IoT architecture, threatening core security goals by enabling various targeted attacks. In the sequel, in accordance with Fig. 2.2, we examine the security of each layer and categorize their corresponding vulnerabilities.

2.5.1 Device-Based Vulnerabilities

Since a large number of IoT devices operate in an unattended fashion with no or limited tamper resistance policies and methodologies, an attacker could take advantage of physical access to a device to cause damage, alter its services or obtain unlimited access to data stored on its memory. To this end, Wurm et al. [150] performed testing of consumer IoT devices and demonstrated how physical access to the hardware enables an adversary to modify boot parameters, extract the root password, and learn other sensitive/private information. Moreover, the authors executed a successful attempt to modify the ID of a smart meter, thus demonstrating the feasibility and practicality of energy theft. Further, the researchers performed several network attacks to retrieve the update file, taking advantage of the lack of encryption at the device level. The authors pinpointed various security enhancements in an attempt to mitigate some of the demonstrated threats such as blocking access to the Universal Asynchronous Receiver-Transmitter (UART), strengthening password-hashing algorithms, and encrypting the file system. In another work, Trappe et al. [138] highlighted the problem of IoT security in the context of the restricted power of the devices. The authors suggested energy harvesting, from both human-made and natural sources, as a suitable method to empower such devices to adopt complex security mechanisms. Nevertheless, it is known that the IoT paradigm faces various obstacles to harvest energy such as strict safety regulations and radio propagation limitations. The researchers suggested that utilizing the physical layer to support confidentiality could possibly be an opportunity for securing the IoT.

2.5.2 Network-Based Vulnerabilities

A number of research efforts addressed IoT-specific vulnerabilities caused by network or protocol weaknesses. For instance, the ZigBee protocol [44], which is developed for low-rate/low-power wireless sensor and control networks, is built on top of IEEE 802.15.4 and offers a stack profile that defines the network, security, and application layers [39]. ZigBee devices establish secure communications by using symmetric keys while the level of sharing of such keys among nodes depends on the security mode [108]. In this context, Vidgren et al. [143] illustrated how an adversary could compromise ZigBee-enabled IoT devices. Although pre-installation of the keys onto each device for a certain security mode is possible, in reality, the keys are transmitted unencrypted, rendering it feasible to leak sensitive information and to allow an adversary to obtain control over the devices. The authors demonstrated several attacks which aim at either gaining control or conducting denial of service on IoT. The researchers suggested that applying the "High-Security" level along with pre-installation of the keys would support the protection of sensitive information, which is essential especially for safety-critical devices. In alternative work, Morgner et al. [90] investigated the security of ZigBee Light Link (ZLL)-based lighting systems. In particular, the authors examined a touchlink commissioning procedure, which is precisely developed to meet requirements of connected light systems. This procedure is responsible for initial device setting within the network and managing network features such as communication between a bulb and a remote control. The authors demonstrated several possible attacks and evaluated their impact by adopting a tailored testing framework. They further pinpointed numerous critical features which affect the security state. In particular, insufficiency of key management and physical protection of the IoT device were elaborated; the former suffers from two significant drawbacks related to sharing pre-defined keys among manufacturers and carrying out the fallback mechanisms. Such observations triggered the interest in the appropriateness of Key Management System (KMS) protocols in the context of the IoT. Accordingly, Roman et al. [115] distinguished four KMS classes: a key pool framework, a mathematical framework, a negotiation framework (i.e., pre-shared key), and a public key framework. By analyzing properties of classes above, the authors concluded that a plethora of traditional protocols is not appropriate due to the unique characteristics demanded from the IoT. Table 2.2 provides a summary of KMS implementation barriers in the context of the IoT. It is worthy to note that the authors analyzed a limited number of scenarios. Thus, further investigation in this area seems to be required.

Likewise, Petroulakis et al. [103] experimentally investigated the correlation between energy consumption and security mechanisms such as encryption, channel assignment, and power control. Table 2.3 presents the summary of their findings, illustrating that the combination of security mechanisms significantly increases energy consumption. Given the energy limitations of the IoT, applying such security methods could lead to energy depletion and hence, affects the availability of the device and its provided services. Although the experiment was restricted to only one IoT device, the XBee Pro, the authors highlighted that the approach could be generic enough to be used to test other devices as well. Auxiliary, Simplicio et al. [131] demonstrated that many of the existing lightweight Authenticated Key Agreement (AKA) schemes suffer from key escrow, which is undesirable in large-scale environments. The authors evaluated escrow-free alternatives to estimate their suitability for IoT. The researchers implemented and benchmarked various schemes and concluded that the Strengthened MQV (SMQV) protocol [121] in combination with implicit certificates avoids transition costs of full-fledged PKI-based certificates, and is a more efficient alternative for other lightweight solutions. Another matter to be considered in the context of network-based weaknesses is related to port blocking policies. To this end, Czyz et al. [32] explored IoT

Table 2.2 Summary of KMS implementation barriers

Protocol framework	Implementation barriers
Key pool framework	Insufficient connectivity
Mathematical framework	Physical distribution of client and server nodes
Negotiation framework	Restricted power of nodes
	Different network residence of client and server nodes
Public key framework	Insufficient security for some cases

Table 2.3 Effect of various security mechanisms on energy consumption

Security mechanism	Effect on energy consumption
Encryption	⇑ 15–30%
Channel assignment	⇑ 10%
Power control	⇑ 4%
All three above	⇑ 230%

connectivity over IPv4 and IPv6 and indicated several insightful findings. The authors noted that a significant number of IoT hosts are only reachable over IPv6 and that various IoT protocols are more accessible on IPv6 than on IPv4. In particular, the researchers pinpointed that the exposure of the Telnet service in 46% of the cases was greater over IPv6 than over IPv4. The authors further contacted IoT network operators to confirm the findings and unveiled that many default port openings are unintentional, which questions IoT security at large.

2.5.3 Software-Based Vulnerabilities

Attackers can also gain remote access to smart IoT nodes by exploiting software vulnerabilities. Such a possibility prompted the research community to investigate this matter. For instance, Angrishi [6] explored IoT-centric malware, which recruited IoT devices into botnets for conducting DDoS attacks. The researcher uncovered that 90% of investigated malware injected default or weak user credentials, while only 10% exploited software-specific weaknesses. Indeed, over the years, the issue of insufficient authentication remains unaddressed, rendering contemporary IoT devices vulnerable to many attacks. We illustrate this issue throughout the past 10 years in Fig. 2.3. A similar conclusion was reached by Markowsky et al. [84]. Referring to the Carna botnet [7], the author noted that it unveiled more than 1.6 million devices throughout the world that used default credentials.

Auxiliary, Patton et al. [101] analyzed CPS. The authors employed the search engine Shodan [127] to index IoT devices that have been deployed in critical infrastructure. The researchers subsequently executed queries with default credentials to gain access to the devices. The authors' experimentation revealed that for various types of IoT, the magnitude of weak password protection varies from 0.44% (Niagara CPS Devices which are widely used in energy management systems) to 40% (traffic control cameras) of investigated devices. Although the conducted experiment was done on a small subset of CPS devices, the reported results, nevertheless, highlights the severity of the problem. Similarly, Cui and Stolfo [29] performed an Internet-scale active probing to uncover close to 540,000 embedded devices with default credentials in various realms such as enterprises, government organizations, Internet Service Providers (ISPs), educational institutions, and private networks. The authors revealed that during 4 months, nearly 97% of devices continued to provide access with default credentials. As a strategy to mitigate unauthorized access, the researchers argued that ISPs should be actively involved in the process of updating user credentials, since the majority of vulnerable devices are under their administration. Moreover, the authors noted that efficient host-based protection mechanism should be implemented.

In the context of firmware vulnerabilities, Costin et al. [25] performed a large-scale static analysis of embedded firmware. The authors were able to recover plaintext passwords from almost 55% of retrieved password hashes. They also extracted 109 private RSA key from 428 firmware images and 56 self-signed SSL

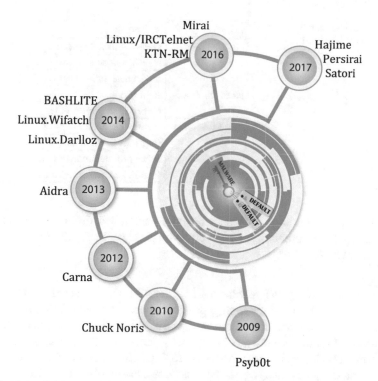

Fig. 2.3 Malware which exploit (IoT) default user credentials

certificates out of 344 firmware images. By searching for such certificates in public ZMap datasets [38], the authors located about 35,000 active devices. Further, the researchers identified recently released firmware which contained kernel versions that are more than 10 years old.

The authors also unveiled that in more than 81% of the cases, web servers were configured to run as privileged users. The authors noted, however, that although the existence of these vulnerabilities seems to be tangible, nonetheless, without the proper hardware, it would be quite impossible to assess the firmware and its susceptibility to exploitations. Additionally, Konstantinou et al. [160] demonstrated how malicious firmware of power grids could corrupt control signals and cause a cascade of power outages. To simulate a firmware integrity attack and analyze its significance, the authors set up a testbed and conducted reverse engineering of the firmware. The researchers pinpointed that some vendors encode public firmware rendering it challenging to an adversary to reverse engineer it. Nevertheless, the authors successfully repackaged the firmware update file and simulated two types of attacks, unveiling that physical damage to the device and voltage instability are two possible drastic consequences.

Table 2.4 IoT vulnerabilities at different architectural layers

Layer	Vulnerabilities
Device-based	Deficient physical security
	Insufficient energy harvesting
	Inadequate authentication
Network-based	Improper encryption
	Unnecessarily open ports
Software-based	Insufficient access control
	Improper patch management capabilities
	Weak programming practices
	Insufficient audit mechanism

To clarify our findings related to the aforementioned discussion, we present Table 2.4, which summarizes IoT vulnerabilities (of Sect. 2.3) based on their architectural layers.

Findings

Indeed, by contrasting IoT architectural layers with the extracted vulnerabilities, we have identified several research gaps. We notice, for instance, that only limited number of IoT devices, their communication protocols, and applications have been assessed from a security point of view, while the research issue on how to extend this knowledge, taking into account IoT-specific traits such as manufacturers, deployment contexts, and types, remains completely obscure. Further, having myriads of authentication protocols, there is a lack of a systematic approach evaluating such protocols in various deployment scenarios. Moreover, while the issue of default credentials have received attention from the operational and research communities, the issue of dealing with significant number of deployed legacy IoT devices (containing hard-coded credentials) undoubtedly still demands additional investigation. Further, in the context of IoT vulnerable programming code, the factors which lead to such insecurities do not seem to have been thoroughly analyzed yet, hindering the realization of proper remediation techniques.

2.6 Security Impact

Given the extracted IoT vulnerabilities, we now elaborate on their impact on core security objectives, namely, confidentiality, integrity, and availability, consistent with the taxonomy of Fig. 2.2.

2.6.1 Confidentiality

This security objective is designed to protect assets from unauthorized access and is typically enforced by strict access control, rigorous authentication procedures, and proper encryption. Nevertheless, the IoT paradigm demonstrates weaknesses in these areas resulting in information leakage. In this context, Copos et al. [23] illustrated how network traffic analysis of IoT thermostats and smoke detectors could be used to learn sensitive information. The authors demonstrated that this knowledge not only hinders the confidentiality of the inhabitants but could also potentially be utilized for unauthorized access to the facilities/homes. The authors captured network traffic generated by the IoT Nest Thermostat and Nest Protect devices, decrypted WPA encryption, and investigated connection logs. Further, they unveiled that although the traffic is encrypted, the devices still reveal destination IP addresses and communication packet sizes that could be successfully used to fingerprint occurring activities. As a simplistic countermeasure, the authors suggested generating same size and length packets and transmitting all the communications through a proxy server. Alternatively, Ronen and Shamir [117] analyzed the leakage of sensitive information such as WiFi passwords and encryption primitives by simulating attacks on smart IoT light bulbs. The researchers pinpointed that during the installation of the smart bulbs, WiFi passwords are transmitted unencrypted, rendering it possible to infer them for malicious purposes. To reduce the risk of information leakage, the authors recommended conducting penetration testing during the design phase, employing standardized and vetted protocols, and forcing authenticated API calls. Further, Wang et al. [146] demonstrated how the combination of motion signals leaked from wearable IoT devices and patterns in the English language allows an adversary to guess a typed text, including credentials. Similarly, the authors in [145] captured motion signals of wearable devices, extracted unique movement patterns, and estimated hand gestures during key entry (input) activities. The authors thus demonstrated that it is feasible to reveal a secret PIN sequence of key-based security systems, which included ATM and electronic door entries. The authors pinpointed that such type of analysis does not require any training or contextual information, making it quite simple for a malicious actor to learn sensitive information. The researchers noted that increasing robustness of the encryption scheme and injecting fabricated noise could possibly prevent such misdemeanors. Additionally, Sachidananda et al. [119] conducted penetration testing, fingerprinting, process enumeration, and vulnerability scanning of numerous consumer IoT devices. The authors' investigation unveiled that a large number of devices have unnecessarily open ports/services, which could be easily leveraged to leak confidential information related to operating systems, device types and transferred data.

2.6.2 Integrity

The integrity objective typically guarantees the detection of any unauthorized modifications and is routinely enforced by strict auditing of access control, rigorous hashing and encryption primitives, interface restrictions, input validations, and intrusion detection methods. However, various unique attributes of the IoT hinder the implementation of sufficient security mechanisms, causing numerous integrity violations against data and software. To this end, Ur et al. [139] investigated ownership rules, roles, and integrity monitoring capabilities of numerous types of home automation devices. The authors pinpointed various access control issues such as insufficiency of audit mechanisms and ability to evade the applied integrity rules. In particular, the researchers highlighted the inability to trace conducted activities and their sources. In addition, Ho et al. [65] investigated a number of integrity attacks such as state consistency events by studying smart IoT lock systems. The authors demonstrated how network architectures, trust models, and reply activities could unlock the door, allowing unauthorized physical access. Moreover, the authors noted that most of the investigated devices do not provide access to integrity logging procedures, rendering it possible for tailored integrity violations to be executed without being noticed. In contrast, Ghena et al. [57] performed security evaluation of wireless traffic signals. The assessment was executed through attack simulations, aiming to exploit a remote access function of the controller. The authors noted that because of the lack of encryption along with the usage of default credentials, an adversary could gain control over the traffic cyber-infrastructure. To this end, an attacker could be able to change the timing of the traffic lights; altering minimum and maximum time for each state and switching or freezing the state of a particular traffic light. These attacks undeniably cause disruptions and safety degradations. The researchers, nevertheless, pinpointed that the Malfunction Management Unit (MMU) typically maintains safety by switching the controller to a known-safe mode in case of a detected integrity violation. The authors attested that, the employment of encryption on the wireless network, regularly updating device firmware, blocking unnecessary network traffic, and changing the default credentials on the operated devices would increase the security of the transport infrastructure. In an alternative work, Takeoglu et al. [134] conducted an experimental investigation of the security and privacy of a cloud-based wireless IP camera. The results demonstrated how elevated permissions of a user permitted root access to the file system, causing numerous integrity violations such as deleting or modifying files. The authors noted that auditing mechanisms and restricting administrator access would contribute to better device security, thus reducing integrity issues.

2.6.3 Availability

This security objective is designed to guarantee timely access to a plethora of resources (including data, applications and network infrastructure) and is often enforced by monitoring and adapting the handling capabilities of such assets, implementing redundancy mechanisms, maintaining backup systems and applying effective security policies and software (or firmware) update patches. Nevertheless, these mechanisms are not always adopted by the IoT. In this context, Costa et al. [24] discussed two groups of availability issues associated with wireless visual sensor networks. These include hardware and coverage failures. While the first group deals with issues such as damage devices, energy depletion and nodes' disconnection, the second group refers to the quality of the information transmitted by the device. Further, Schuett et al. [122] demonstrated how firmware modifications could hamper the availability of IoT devices deployed in critical infrastructure. The authors repackaged firmware images, so they trigger a termination signal, ceasing the operation of the device or restricting the owners' access to such devices. The researchers conducted hardware analysis to identify the employed instructions used in the firmware images. To this end, they enumerated their sub-functions to perform tailored modifications, aiming at designing a number of attacks. The authors demonstrated the impact of remote termination commands, which as noted by the authors, could be relatively easily mitigated by updating the firmware. The authors concluded by stating that mapping firmware images to protected memory and digitally signing firmware updates could increase the efforts of an adversary, thus reducing the risk of such availability attacks. Moreover, recently, the U.S. Department of Homeland Security (DHS) had issued an alert [140] notifying IoT operators and users about the rise of permanent DoS attacks, which target devices with default credentials and open Telnet ports. In this sense, an attacker could disrupt device functions by corrupting its storage. DHS noted that mitigation strategies include changing the default credentials, disabling Telnet access and employing server clusters which are able to handle large network traffic.

Given the aforementioned information, which interplay IoT vulnerabilities with their impacted security objectives, we present Table 2.5 which summarizes IoT vulnerabilities in the context of their attack vectors and security objectives. Such summary would be of interest to readers that are aiming to comprehend what has been accomplished already to address such IoT vulnerabilities and would facilitate IoT research initiation in the highlighted areas.

Findings
We observe the absence of studies which measure the effect of violations of various security objectives in different deployment domains. Indeed, a confidentiality breach in the context of light bulbs is not as critical as in the context of medical devices. Such intelligence would prioritize the remediation depending on the deployment domain. Further, while weak programming practices have a significant security impact, we notice the shortage of research work which systematically assess how such practices violate different security objectives in the context of

Table 2.5 Security impact of IoT vulnerabilities

Layer	Vulnerabilities	Security impact[a]			References
		C	I	A	
Device-based	Deficient physical security		✓	✓	[24, 121, 138, 149]
	Insufficient energy harvesting			✓	[24, 55, 137]
	Inadequate authentication	✓	✓		[23, 64, 89, 102, 114, 130, 142]
Network-based	Improper encryption	✓	✓		[56, 116, 144, 145]
	Unnecessarily open ports	✓		✓	[32, 118, 139]
	Insufficient access control	✓	✓	✓	[6, 25, 29, 56, 83, 100, 133, 138, 139]
Software-based	Improper patch management capabilities			✓	[25, 71, 121]
	Weak programming practices	✓	✓		[25]
	Insufficient audit mechanism		✓		[64, 138]

[a] *C* confidentiality, *I* integrity, *A* availability

IoT. Moreover, we infer the lack of studies analyzing the efficiency of IoT audit mechanisms. Indeed, exploring existing audit mechanisms along with assessing their robustness in the context of different IoT devices under various deployment environments would provide valuable insights and would enable the development of proper mitigation strategies.

2.7 Attacks

After elaborating on the relationships between IoT vulnerabilities, their attack vectors from an architectural perspective and their corresponding impacted security objectives, we now discuss literature-extracted IoT attacks, which tend to exploit such vulnerabilities, as illustrated in the taxonomy of Fig. 2.2.

2.7.1 Attacks Against Confidentiality and Authentication

The primary goal of this class of attack is to gain unauthorized access to IoT resources and data to conduct further malicious actions. This type of attack is often induced by executing brute force events, evesdropping IoT physical measurements, or faking devices identities.

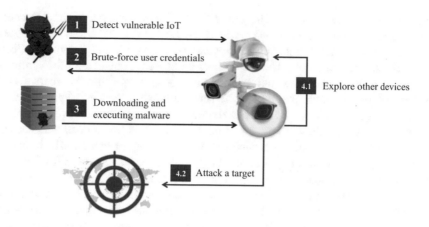

Fig. 2.4 Mirai attack process

Broadly, *dictionary attacks* aim at gaining access to IoT devices through executing variants of brute force events, leading to illicit modifications of settings or even full control of device functions. In this context, very recently, Antonakakis et al. [8] illustrated how a dictionary attack could compromise millions of Internet-connected devices and turn them into a malicious army to launch orchestrated attacks against core Internet services. The authors analyzed over 1000 malware variants to document the evolution of the Mirai malware, learn its detection avoidance techniques and uncover its targets. By monitoring requests to a network telescope (i.e., a set of routable, allocated yet unused IP addresses) and employing filters to distinguish Mirai traffic, the authors identified 1.2 million Mirai infected IP addresses associated with various deployment environments and types of IoT devices. Figure 2.4 illustrates a summary of this attack. The infection mechanism was executed in various phases, including rapid scanning for target identification, brute-force logins for learning the device operating settings, and downloading architecture-specific malware for exploitation and usage. Further, *side-channel attacks* (i.e., power analysis) endeavor to recover devices cryptographic keys by leveraging existing correlations between physical measurements and the internal states of IoT devices [161]. This attack consists of two phases, namely, information acquisition and correlation analysis. In the former step, an adversary observes the associations between a number of physical attributes such as power consumption and electromagnetic emission for different inputs parameters. Such correlations are typically referred to as side-channel information and could be exploited for malicious purposes. To evaluate the method of physically measuring power, O'Flynn and Chen [96] inserted a resistive shunt into the power supply of the targeted IoT wireless node, which uses the IEEE802.15.4 protocol. The captured power traces were then used for detecting the location of software encryption and for recovering the respective encryption key. The authors noted that this attack is quite hard to detect because the captured node is absent in the network for only a short time.

Similarly, Biryukov et al. [15] illustrated a vulnerability related to the Advanced Encryption Standard (AES), which is widely used in the IEEE802.15.4 protocol as a building block for encryption, and authentication messages in IoT communications. To assess the resiliency of AES, the authors employed an algorithm for symbolic processing of the cipher state and described an optimal algorithm that recovers the master key. In particular, the researchers showed how a protected implementation of AES based on S-box and T-table strategies could be broken even when an adversary controls a limited amount of information. Additionally, an attacker can manipulate the identity of compromised devices aiming to maliciously influence the network. To this end, Rajan et al. [110] modeled *sybil attacks* in IoT context and evaluated the impact on the network performance. The authors defined two types of sybil identities and labeled them as stolen and fabricated identities. The researchers implemented the malicious behavior of nodes with such fake identities. In particular, they evaluated the performance of the network when packets are dropped or selective forwarded. Based on behavioral profiling of IoT devices, the authors proposed a detection technique rooted in trust relationship between nodes.

Examples of Real Attacks Against Confidentiality

2016:   Mirai botnet [8]
        BrickerBot [109]
        IoT toys leaking millions of voice messages [49]

2.7.2 Attacks Against Data Integrity

The sabotage of IoT data is also quite damaging to the IoT paradigm. Attacks against integrity are prompted by injection of false data or modification of device firmware.

False Data Injection (FDI) attacks fuse legitimate or corrupted input towards IoT sensors to cause various integrity violations. For instance, lunching such attacks could mislead the state estimation process of a IoT device, causing dramatic economic impact or even loss of human life [78]. In this context, Liu et al. [81] simulated data injection attacks on power utilities. The authors investigated the scenarios in which an attacker aims to inject random measurements to IoT sensors. In particular, this work pinpointed the severity of such attack class by revealing that an attacker would only need to compromise 1% of the IoT meters in the system to severely threaten the resiliency of the entire power grid. The authors pinpointed several requirements for conducting such an attack, including, a thorough knowledge of the systems' dynamics, and the ability to manipulate the measurements before they are used for state estimation. Although these requirements seem to be challenging to achieve, the authors report several cases which prove that that such requirements do not prevent the accomplishment of the attack, leading to catastrophic negative impacts. In a closely related work, Liu et al. [80] proposed and validated numerous strategies which allows the proper execution of FDI attacks, with limited network information while maintaining stealthiness. To this end, the authors examined network characteristics of an IoT-empowered power grid and built a linear programming model that minimized the number of required measurements. The researchers conducted various experiments rooted in emulation studies to validate their model. Another category of attacks, namely, *firmware modification*, is rendered by malicious alteration of the firmware, which induces a functional disruption of the targeted device. Figure 2.5 depicts the attacks' three-step procedure; reconnaissance, reverse engineering, and repackaging and uploading. Given the significant negative impact of such attacks on the IoT paradigm, the research community has been quite active in exploring related issues and solutions. For instance, Basnight et al. [13] illustrated how firmware could be maliciously modified and uploaded to an Allen-Bradley ControlLogix which is Programmable Logic Controller (PLC). By conducting reverse engineering, the authors were able to initially learn the functionality of the firmware update mechanism to subsequently modify the configuration file, rendering it possible to inject malicious code into a firmware update. The authors pinpointed that the resource limitation of PLC devices hinders the implementation of a robust algorithm that would attempt to verify data integrity. In alternative work, Cui et al. [28] analyzed a large number of LaserJet printer firmware and executed firmware modification attacks by reverse engineering a number of hardware components. The authors identified over 90,000 unique, vulnerable printers that are publicly accessible over the Internet. The authors alarmed that such devices were located in governmental and military organizations, educational institutions, ISPs, and private

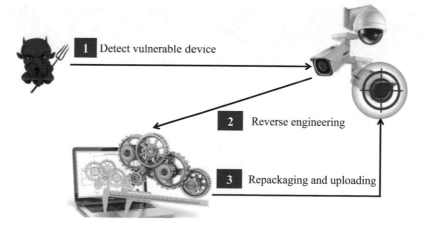

Fig. 2.5 Stages of firmware modification attack

corporations. The researchers unveiled that many firmware are released with known vulnerabilities and about 80% of firmware images rely on third-party libraries that contain known vulnerabilities. Moreover, the authors noted that update mechanisms typically do not require authentication, facilitating a firmware modification attack. In addition, the researchers stated that the rate of current IoT firmware patches is significantly low, noting that 25% of the patched printers do not address the default user credentials' issue. The authors also pinpointed the lack of IoT host-based defense/integrity mechanisms, which can prevent firmware modification attacks. Auxiliary, Konstantinou and Maniatakos [72] defined firmware modifications as a new class of cyber-physical attacks against the IoT paradigm (within the context of a smart grid) and illustrated how an adversary could disrupt an operation of circuit breakers by injecting malicious tripping commands to the relay controllers. By conducting reverse engineering, the authors determined the details of the operating system, extracted the functionality of various critical routines, and located key structures to be modified. The analysis of the obtained files exposed passwords of a large number of deployed IoT devices and disclosed the encryption key. The authors further uploaded a modified firmware to an embedded device and revealed that the update validation employed a simplistic checksum which can be easily circumvented. The researchers analyzed different attack scenarios and concluded that maliciously modified IoT firmware could indeed cause a cascade of power outages within the context of the smart grid. Further, Bencsath et al. [14] introduced a general framework for Cross-Channel Scripting (CCS) attacks targeting IoT embedded software, proved its feasibility by implementing it on Planex wireless routers, and demonstrated how this vulnerability could create an entry point to install malicious code to turn the devices into bots in coordinated botnets. The framework consisted of three stages, namely, vulnerability exploitation, platform identification, and malicious firmware updates. Through this, the authors highlighted the feasibility of CCS attacks targeting the IoT paradigm.

Example of Real Attack Against Integrity
2015: Baby monitor "converses" to children[27]

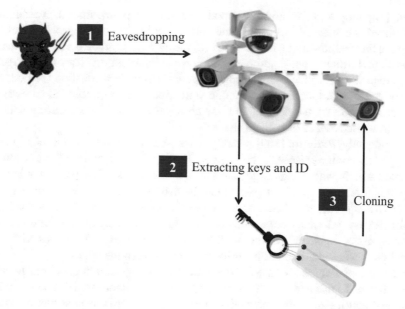

Fig. 2.6 Node capturing attack phases

2.7.3 Attacks Against Availability

The primary goal of Denial of Service (DoS) attacks against IoT is to prevent the legitimate users' timely access to IoT resources (i.e., data and services). This type of attack is often induced by revoking device from the network or draining IoT resources until their full exhaustion.

As noted earlier, IoT devices typically reside in unattended and physically unprotected realms. In this context, an adversary could capture, alter or destroy a device to retrieve stored sensitive information, including secret keys. We label this group of attacks, following literature terminology, as *device capture*. In this context, Smache et al. [132] formalized a model for node capturing attacks, given a secure IoT WSN. The authors defined the attack as consisting of a combination of passive, active, and physical attack events that is executed by an intelligent adversary. Figure 2.6 illustrates such misdemeanor by highlighting its three phases.

This attack includes (1) eavesdropping and selecting victim nodes, during which an attacker investigates the network to identify a suitable target, (2) extracting sensitive information, and (3) cloning a node. The authors also assessed the capability of an intrusion detection system in detecting such malicious behaviors by monitoring incoming network packets as well as monitoring device memory. Further, Zhao [159] analyzed the resiliency to node-capture attacks of random key pre-distribution IoT schemes, namely, the q-composite extension of the scheme proposed by Eschenauer and Gligor in [42], and provided several design guidelines for secure sensor networks by employing such scheme. In auxiliary work, Bonaci et al. [16] proposed an adversary model of node capture attacks. The authors formulated the network security issue into a control theoretic problem set. By applying this framework to an IoT network, the authors simulated and analyzed the network performance and stability under physical intervention. They also proposed (1) an algorithm for identifying corrupted nodes, (2) node revocation methods and (3) key refreshment techniques for node validation. Although this model does not protect IoT node from being captured by an adversary, it allows securing network from the consequences of such an attack.

Additionally, Radware [109] recently witnessed and alarmed about nearly 2000 attempts to compromise IoT honeypots. Further investigation of such attacks unveiled that it was designed to damage the devices, so that the latter become inoperable. A study of this attack, which the authors labeled as Permanent Denial of Service (PDoS), revealed that an adversary exploited default credentials and performed several Linux commands that led to storage corruptions, Internet connectivity disruptions, and wiping of all files on the devices. IoT devices with open Telnet ports were identified as the primary target of such the attack.

Further, *sinkhole attacks* modify the network topology and degrade IoT network performance. To this end, the attacker empowers the malicious nodes with the ability to advertise artificial routing paths to include as many nodes as possible in order to oblige them to send packets through such bogus paths. The malicious node than either drop or selective forwards the information. By simulating a sinkhole attack in an 6LoWPAN IoT network, Wallgren et al. [144] observed huge traffic passing through the attacker nodes. It is worthy to pinpoint that coupled with other attacks, sinkhole attacks would cause more significant harm for routing protocols.

Also known as vampire attacks, the *batarry draining attacks* are broadly defined by Vasserman and Hopper [142] as the transmission of a message (or a datagram) in a way which demands significantly more energy from the network and its nodes to be employed and acted upon in contrast with typical messages. The authors in [142] evaluated two subtypes of such attacks, namely, *carousel* and *stretch attacks*. On one hand, carousel attacks permit an adversary to send messages as a series of loops such that the same node appears in the route several times. On the other hand, stretch attacks allow malicious nodes to artificially construct long routes so that the packets traverse through a larger, inversely optimal number of IoT nodes. Conducted simulations illustrated that a given network under such attacks increase its energy consumption up to 1000% depending on the location of the adversary. The authors pinpointed that the combination of these attacks could tremendously increases the level of consumed power, and thus, drain energy quite promptly. The researchers attested that carousel attacks could be prevented by validating source routes for loops and discarding nodes which have initially sent such messages. In case of stateful protocols, which are typically network topology-aware, the attacks mentioned here become relatively limited.

Besides, Pielli et al. [104] investigated *jamming attacks*, which aim at disrupting IoT network communications and reducing the lifetime of energy-constrained nodes by creating interference and causing packet collisions. By leveraging a game theoretic approach, the authors studied jamming attack scenarios in the context of various strategies. The results demonstrated a trade-off between communication reliability and device lifetime. Nevertheless, jamming is a severe problem in the IoT context, especially that legacy nodes are inherently vulnerable to such attacks.

> **Example of Real Attack Against Availability**
> 2016: Cold Finland [87]

Given the aforementioned information, which elaborates on literature-extracted attacks that could possibly exploit the IoT vulnerabilities as pinpointed in Sect. 2.3, we now present Table 2.6 which summarizes the relationship between the detailed attacks and targeted vulnerabilities.

Findings
We note the shortage of research works devoted to studying IoT-specific attacks, given that many contributions have been dedicated to addressing the issue of threat classifications in WSN. We also observe that the same attacks could exploit various vulnerabilities of IoT paradigm, rather than targeting only one of them. In this context, dictionary, firmware modification, and device capturing attacks render the most severe damage. Further, we notice the deficiency of endeavors that aim at generating tangible notions of IoT maliciousness, especially that intrusion detection techniques would highly benefit from such knowledge.

2.8 Remediation

Coherent with the taxonomy of Fig. 2.2, IoT vulnerabilities can further be classified by their corresponding remediation strategies. We distinguish three classes of such strategies, namely, access and authentication controls, software assurance, and security protocols. We elaborate on their details in the sequel.

2.8.1 Access and Authentication Controls

To address a number of IoT vulnerabilities, authentication and authorization techniques are typically adopted. Nevertheless, given the low computational power of IoT devices, such mechanisms continue to be challenged in such contexts. However, there has been some recent attempts to address this. To this end, Hafeez et al. [63] proposed Securebox, a platform for securing IoT networks. The platform provides a number of features including device isolation in addition to vetting device to device communications. The platform intercepts any connection request from a connected IoT device to a remote destination and subsequently verifies if various security

Table 2.6 Attacks targeting IoT paradigm

Vulnerability	Dictionary attack	Side-channel attack	Sybil attack	False data injection	Firmware modification	Device capturing	Sinkhole attack	Battery draining attack	Jamming attack	References
Deficient physical security		✓			✓	✓				[13–16, 28, 71, 95, 131, 158]
Insufficient energy harvesting							✓	✓	✓	[103, 141, 143]
Inadequate authentication			✓	✓		✓	✓			[8, 16, 70, 79, 80, 86, 109, 131, 143, 158]
Improper encryption		✓								[15, 95]
Unnecessarily open ports	✓									[108]
Insufficient access control	✓									[8, 108]
Improper patch management capabilities					✓					[13, 14, 28, 71]
Weak programming practices	✓			✓	✓					[8, 13, 14, 28, 71, 79, 80]
Insufficient audit mechanism	✓			✓	✓	✓				[8, 13, 14, 16, 28, 71, 79, 80, 158]

policies match the requested connection. When a suspicious activity is detected, the platform quarantines such attempt and alarms the user in an attempt to provide cyber security awareness. Nonetheless, the proposed solution is still theoretical and indeed requires thorough empirical experimentation. In contrast, Qabulio et al. [107] proposed a generic framework for securing mobile wireless IoT networks against physical attacks. In particular, the authors leveraged messages directed towards the base station to infer spoofed/cloned nodes. The authors proposed techniques by exploiting time differences in inter-arrival rate to detect spoofed packets. The proposed framework was successfully tested by employing the Contiki OS [36] and the COOJA simulator [93]. In alternative work, Hei et al. [64] proposed a lightweight security scheme to defend against resource depletion attacks. By employing Support Vector Machines (SVM) to explore patterns generated by Implantable Medical Devices (IMD), the authors throttled malicious authentications, thus saving a significant amount of energy related to the IMD. The researchers achieved a notable accuracy for detecting unauthorized access attempts; 90% and 97% accuracy for linear and non-linear SVM classifiers, respectively. Given that the proposed scheme employs a smartphone as a mechanism to conduct classification, it might have some issues if the smartphone is stolen or forgotten by the patient. In this case, it is unclear how access will be granted. Further, the proposed scheme was designed and tested only on one type of IoT device and thus might not be generic enough to be employed for various IoT types. Similarly, Yang et al. [151] proposed an RFID-based solution aiming to address several IoT security challenges such as device authentication, confidentiality, and integrity of devices through their supply chain. Indeed, on the way from the manufacturer to the end users, the devices or their components could be stolen, replaced by malicious ones or modified. By binding the RFID tags with the control chip of the IoT devices, the authors aimed to prevent these situations. To this end, the solution indexes the following traces: (1) unique combination of tag and device IDs, (2) session keys, and (3) the supply path. The verification of these traces ensures that the IoT devices were not replaced by fake ones. Although the proposed solution holds promise to provide security through the supply chain, it is still in its design phase and ultimately requires thorough evaluation. Further, by adopting the Constrained Application Protocol (CoAP), Jan et al. [68] proposed a lightweight authentication algorithm for verifying IoT devices' identities before running them in an operational network. In particular, the authors argued that using a single key for authentication purposes reduces connection overheads and computational load. By limiting the number of allowed connections for each ID to a single one, the authors aimed to restrict multiple connections between malicious nodes and servers at a given time, hence, protecting the network against a plethora of attacks such as eavesdropping, key fabrication, resource exhaustion and denial of service. However, the proposed algorithm does not defend the IoT network if the malicious node actively spoofs multiple identities. In alternate work, Kothmayr et al. [73] introduced a two-way authentication scheme for the IoT paradigm based on the Datagram Transport Layer Security (DTLS) [114] protocol. The scheme is suggested to be deployed between the transport and application layers. The evaluation of the proposed mechanism in a real IoT testbed demonstrated its feasibility and applicability in various IoT settings. Further, Sciancalepore et al. [123] presented a Key Management Service (KMS) protocol that employs certificates, by applying the Elliptic Curve Qu-Vanstone (ECQV) [21] algorithm. The evaluation results demonstrated that the approach demands low bandwidth and reasonable ROM footprint. Although the algorithm can be considered applicable to the IoT paradigm, the authors did not assess its security under various IoT settings. Moreover, the employed certificates require secure management and the authors did not clarify how to satisfy this requirement. Along the same line of thought, Porambage et al. [105] introduced a lightweight authentication mechanism, namely PAuthKey, for WSNs in distributed IoT applications, which aimed at ensuring end-to-end security and reliable data transmission. Besides this, Park et al. [98] proposed a more complex solution. The authors adopted ECQV [21] certificates and employed the concept of Cryptographically Generated Address (CGA) [11]. The integration of this combination into the existing IEEE 802.15.4 [89] protocol indeed yielded promising results. In particular, in contrast to PAuthKey [105], the proposed scheme required less energy and execution time. Likewise, Garcia-Morchon et al. [54] proposed two security architectures by adapting the DTLS [114] and the HIP [92] protocols for IoT devices with Pre-Shared Keys (PSK). The schemes' evaluations demonstrated that authentication based on DTLS negatively affects network performance and thus performs much worse than HIP-based authentication. In particular, DTLS induces a larger memory footprint while HIP added significant overhead in the context of key management. Both designs aimed to achieve several security features such as mutual authentication between the IoT device and the domain manager, assurance of legitimate access to the network, and enforcement of standardized communication protocols.

Alternatively, many researchers concentrated on biometric-based access control. Biometrics often refers to various characteristics such as fingerprints, iris, voice, and heartbeat. In this context, Rostami et al. [118] introduced an access-control policy, namely Heart-to-heart, for IMD. The policy offers a compelling balance between resistance against a number of attacks and level of accessibility/usability in an emergency situation. Specifically, the researchers proposed a lightweight authentication protocol which exploits Electrocardiography (ECG) randomness to defend against active attacks. Following an emerging trend rendered by the adoption of biometrics for authentication, Hossain et al. [66] presented an infrastructure for an end-to-end secure solution based on biometric characteristics. The proposed architecture consists of four layers. These include IoT devices, communication, cloud, and application. The sensors collect biometric features and transmit them through encrypted communication channels to a cloud, where they are processed by the application layer. The authors illustrated prevention methods against numerous attacks such as replication attacks, in which an attacker copies data from one session to be employed in a new session. Similarly, Guo et al. [62] noted that traditional access control such as a passwords is outdated. The authors proposed an access control approach which includes biometric-based key generation; a robust technique against reverse engineering and unauthorized access. To protect biometric information, the authors suggested to employ an additional chip that acts as a permutation block, in order to permit secure communications between programmable and non-programmable components. Executed simulation results exhibited reliability characteristics and a relatively small amount of information leakage. The authors attested that such an approach for authentication could also enhance IoT applications by, for instance, extracting gender and age information from biometrics and generating relevant statistics, or maintaining public safety by promptly identifying illegitimate individuals. In the same way, Dhillon et al. [34] proposed a lightweight multi-factor authentication protocol to elevate the security of the IoT. The proposed scheme employs a gateway node which requires the user to register prior to initiating any communication. To this end, a user generates their identity, credentials, personal biometric traits, and a random number. The combination of these features create a hash value, which is used for authentication. Once registered, the user can demand access through a smart device by logging in to the desired IoT service/application using their biometrics and credentials. Security is enforced by utilizing one-way hash, perceptual hash functions, and XOR operations that are computationally less expensive and, thus, suitable in IoT environments. Evaluation of this approach demonstrated that the proposed access method considerably limits information leakage in case of physical, denial-of-service and replay attacks. Nevertheless, complexity analysis of the proposed scheme should be conducted to strongly validate its applicability for resource-constrained IoT devices.

In addition, few research contributions have been dedicated to context-aware permission models. For instance, Jia et al. [69] aimed to design a context-based permission system that captures environmental IoT contexts, analyze previous security-relevant details, and take further mitigative action. To this end, the authors conducted an extensive analysis of possible intrusion scenarios and designed a method which fingerprints attack contexts within certain IoT applications. In a similar context, Fernandes et al. [46] introduced a method of restricting access to sensitive IoT data. The authors designed a system dubbed as FlowFence, which allows controlling the way data is used by the application. The researchers achieved this goal by granting access to sensitive data only to user-defined data flow patterns while blocking all undefined flows. The proposed solution empowers developers with the ability to split their application into two modules; the first module operates sensitive IoT information in a sandbox, while the second component coordinates the transmission of such sensitive data by employing integrity constraints. The validation of FlowFence in a consumer IoT realm demonstrated the preservation of confidential information, with limited increase in overhead. Besides academic research, security vendors are also introducing smart security solutions. Among those, Dojo [19], Cujo [31], Rattrap [67], and Luma [82] stand out and provide network security services for IoT in home and critical CPS environments. Their features include firewall capabilities, secure web proxy, and intrusion detection and prevention systems. Although these products promise to protect home networks with little effort from the user, their configuration settings are not always straight forward, often resembling a black-box solution, while their evaluation in real IoT realms has not been exhaustively reported.

2.8.2 Software Assurance

Given the potential impact of exploiting IoT software, the proper software assurance ought to be an integral part of the development life-cycle. This aims at reducing the vulnerabilities of both source and binary code to provide resiliency to the IoT paradigm. To this end, Costin el al. [26] proposed a scalable, automated framework for dynamic analysis aiming to discover vulnerabilities within embedded IoT firmware images. The authors performed their investigation by emulating firmware and adapting available free penetration tools such as Arachni [120], Zed Attack Proxy (ZAP) [95] and w3af [5]. By testing close to 2000 firmware images, the authors discovered that nearly 10% of them contains vulnerabilities such as command injection and cross-channel scripting. Further, Li et al. [75] noted that traditional code verification techniques lack domain-specificity, which is crucial in IoT contexts, notably for embedded medical devices. In particular, the authors pinpointed that delays in code execution paths could threaten the life of an individual. However, currently available techniques do not verify the delays. With the aim to improve the trustworthiness of the software embedded in medical devices, the authors proposed to extend traditional code verification techniques by fusing safety-related properties of specific medical device to code model checker such as CBMC [86]. To this end, the researchers transformed safety properties to testable assertions against which the checker verifies the programming code. The implementation of the proposed techniques for the software verification of pacemaker, which is implantable electronic device that regulates heartbeats, unveiled that the software code failed various safety properties.

Applying the aforementioned and similar techniques aims at finding vulnerabilities without executing software code, thus requiring access to source code. The assessment of binary code, on the other hand, is more applicable when programming code is not available. Many traditional techniques could be adopted for the IoT paradigm. For instance, Zaddach et al. [155] presented a framework dubbed as Avatar for dynamic analysis of embedded IoT systems by utilizing an emulator and a real IoT device. In particular, an emulator executes firmware code, where any Input/Output (IO) is forwarded to the physical device. Consequently, signals and interrupts are collected on the device and injected back into the emulator. An evaluation of the framework proved its capability to assist in IoT security-related firmware assessment; reverse engineering, vulnerability discovery and hard-coded backdoor detection. Alternatively, Feng at al. [45] demonstrated how learning of high-level features of a control flow graph could improve the performance of firmware vulnerability search methods. The proposed approach employs unsupervised learning methods to identify control flow graph features extracted from a binary function. Such features are then transformed into a numeric vector for applying Locality Sensitive Hashing (LSH). By leveraging a method rooted in visual information retrieval to optimize the performance of the vulnerability search mechanism, the authors demonstrated the efficiency and accuracy of the proposed scheme. Moreover, an analysis of more than 8000 IoT firmware unveiled that many of them are vulnerable to known OpenSSL vulnerabilities, opening the door for DoS attacks and leakage of sensitive information. Along the same line, Elmiligi et al. [40] introduced a multidimensional method to analyze embedded systems security at different levels of abstraction. The foundation of the approach is mapping the attacks to three dimensions, namely, programming level, integration level, and a life cycle phase. This permitted the capability to analyze more than 25 IoT-centric security scenarios. The authors illustrated how the proposed evaluation methodology indeed improves the security of IoT embedded systems during various product life-cycles.

2.8.3 Security Protocols

Zhang et al. [157] argued that enclosing each node in tamper-resistant hardware is unrealistic and cost inefficient. With the aim to design an energy efficient and compromise-tolerant scheme, Zhang et al. proposed the Coverage Interface Protocol (CIP). The authors advocated that the proposed protocol can protect a device from both, external physical attacks and attacks originating from compromised nodes. The CIP consists of two components, namely, a Boundary Node Detection scheme (BOND) and a Location-Based Symmetric Key management protocol (LBSK). BOND equips IoT nodes with the ability to recognize their boundary nodes, while LBSK establishes related keys to secure core network operations. While the proposed scheme seems to be efficient by saving energy, its large-scale evaluation in a real IoT testbed would definitely aid in realizing its advantages and disadvantages. Alternatively, Rao et al. [111] proposed the predictive node expiration-based, energy-aware source routing protocol, which attempts to optimize the overall energy efficiency of the IoT sensor network. This aims at ensuring that the sensed information effectively reaches the sink through a reliable path. Further, Glissa and Meddeb [58] considered various potential attacks on 6LoWPAN and proposed a multi-layered security protocol, namely, the Combined 6LoWPSec. The proposed scheme aimed at limiting attacks on IPv6 IoT communications. By leveraging security features of IEEE 802.15.4, the authors designed an algorithm which operates at the MAC layers. In contrast to gathering security-related information at each node hop, the authors proposed approach enables security implementation at the device level. Evaluation of 6LoWPSec demonstrated power efficiency under a number of attack scenarios. Given that IoT applications often utilize the cloud to store and share data, Shafagh et al. [125] approached IoT security by designing a data protection framework, dubbed as Talos, where the cloud curates encrypted data while permitting the execution of specific queries. The proposed solution relied on Partial Homomorphic Encryption (PHE). Through executing micro-benchmarking and system performance evaluation, the authors experimentally demonstrated that the proposed solution consumed modest energy level, while providing a measurable increase in security level. The same researchers extended Talos in [124] and presented a next generation PHE solution for IoT; designed and implemented using additive homomorphic schemes. The proposed protocol is composed of three main building blocks. These include a client engine, a cloud engine, and an identity providers; only the client engine has access to the keying material. This component is also responsible for encryption/decryption, triggering key revocations, and several sharing-related activities. The cloud engine, on the other hand, provides the database interface and features, and only operates on encrypted data. The responsibility to verify user identity is given to the third party identity provider. In the context of implementation, the researchers prototyped their solution for the mobile platform and thoroughly evaluated its inner workings. The authors concluded that the proposed protocol possesses reasonable overhead in processing time and end-to-end latency. Auxiliary, Wei et al. [148] recently offered a scalable, one-time file encryption protocol, which combined robust cryptographic techniques to protect files from arbitrary users. By adopting techniques and technologies rooted in identity-based encryption, the authors designed and implemented a capability to securely transmit key pairs via SSL/TLS channels. Further, Yang et al. [153] proposed a lightweight access protocol for IoT in healthcare. In this context, access to IoT data should be granted in two different situations under usual and emergency modes/situations. In the first mode, the proposed scheme employs attribute-based access, thus family members and health providers would have different privileges. In case of emergency, on the other hand, an emergency contact person utilizes a password to extract a secret key to decrypt patient's medical files. As reported by the authors, the scheme does not leak access-related information, and requires lower communication and computation costs than other existing attribute-based access control schemes in the context of IoT.

Having elaborated on the above, we now summarize the key findings in Table 2.7, which depict the relationship between the extracted IoT vulnerabilities and their corresponding remediation approaches.

Findings
Physical access to IoT devices could ultimately cause their damage, unveiling their cryptographic schemes, replicating them by malicious ones, and corrupting their data. While all the aforementioned issues are quite severe, we notice the lack of their corresponding remediation strategies. Further, while several firewalls are already proposed in the context of the IoT, mostly those that are designed by the industry, it remains unclear whether their marketing hype matches their security expectations. Even though emerging solutions such as biometric and context-aware permission models promise to improve access controls in IoT realms, they undoubtedly raise a number of concerns and issues. Among them, how well the proposed biometric-based access control would maintain the security of the biometrics and to which extent would context-aware permission models be practically implemented. Moreover, both of their large-scale implementation, evaluation and validation in tangible IoT realms require further investigation. Further, although there exists a number of research efforts which propose IoT-tailored encryption schemes, we notice the shortage of studies which exhaustively and thoroughly assess and

Table 2.7 Summary of remediation strategies

Vulnerability	Remediation strategy			References
	Access controls	Software assurance	Security protocols	
Deficient physical security	✓			[106, 150, 156]
Insufficient energy harvesting	✓		✓	[12, 63, 69, 110, 156]
Inadequate authentication	✓			[19, 31, 53, 62, 66, 67, 72, 81, 97, 104, 122, 150]
Improper encryption			✓	[123, 124, 147]
Unnecessarily open ports				–
Insufficient access control	✓	✓	✓	[3, 34, 46, 61, 65, 117, 152]
Improper patch management capabilities				–
Weak programming practices		✓		[26, 40, 45, 74, 154]
Insufficient audit mechanism	✓			[150]

analyze their advantages and disadvantages under different malicious and benign IoT scenarios. We also pinpoint the lack of approaches which aim at overcoming the insufficiency of IoT audit mechanisms in reducing the possibility to conceal the involvement of the IoT in malicious activities. Finally, we note the deficiency of remediation techniques concentrated on unnecessarily open ports and improper patch management. Indeed, such methods would ensure meeting various security objectives, as pinpointed in Table 2.5.

2.9   Situational Awareness Capabilities

Having a myriad of IoT devices with numerous unique traits such as type, manufacturer, firmware version, and context in which they operate in, it is indeed quite challenging to continuously infer evolving IoT-specific vulnerabilities. Moreover, adversaries will continue to became more advanced and skilled, executing sophisticated, stealthy attacks, thus exploiting 0-day and other critical vulnerabilities. To guarantee a certain level of IoT security and resiliency, the effectiveness of any security mechanism would need to be subject to regular assessments and scrutiny. In this context, IoT vulnerabilities, in accordance with the taxonomy of Fig. 2.2, could be further classified by various (operational) security assessments and monitoring strategies. We distinguish four classes of such categories, including, vulnerability assessment techniques, honeypots, network discovery methods, and intrusion detection mechanisms.

2.9.1 Vulnerability Assessment

Executing security evaluations undoubtedly aids in discovering IoT vulnerabilities prior to them being exploited. Various methods ranging from testbeds to attack simulation and fuzzing techniques have been decisive in obtaining effective and actionable information related to the cyber threat posture of the IoT paradigm.

A research direction in this area focuses on designing new testbeds or adopting existing methods to perform IoT vulnerability assessment. One of such testbeds, which utilize a number of open source software such as Kali Linux, Open VAS, Nessus, Nexpose, and bindwalk, was proposed by Tekeoglu et al. [135]. Such proposed approach enables the capturing of network traffic for analyzing its features to identify IoT security vulnerabilities. In particular, the authors noted several insightful inferences; most of the investigated IoT devices do not lock-out users after failed login attempts; several unnecessary open ports facilitate targeted attacks; and a large number of devices are operated with outdated versions of their software and firmware. The authors advocated that the proposed testbed could be leveraged to conduct various experiments. While the testbed seems quite practical, its operating procedure is still rather manual. Further, Siboni et al. [129] designed a unique testbed for wearable devices. The framework performs the traditional vulnerability tests along with security assessments in different contexts, which is crucial and quite practical when dealing with the IoT paradigm. The technical architecture of the proposed testbed consists of various modules; a functional module which is responsible for test management, a module which is tied to the execution of standard security tests, a unit for generating insights related to context-aware assessments, and a module dedicated for the analysis and report generation. Such a layered architecture allows deploying relevant simulators and measurements for a particular IoT device. As a proof-of-concept, the framework was used for different wearable IoT devices such as Google Glass and smartwatch. In another work, Reaves and Morris [113] designed two testbeds for IoT within Industrial Control Systems (ICS) to compare different implementation types and to infer the most efficient way to identify vulnerabilities. One of the testbeds consists of physical devices in a laboratory environment, while the other emulates device behavior using Python scripts. To test the response of the system in cases of adding devices to the network or infiltration of the radio signals, the researchers simulated three kinds of attacks. The authors reported their results by indicating that both implementations efficiently emulate real systems. However, some unique IoT traits, including their manufacturing characteristics, should be tested separately. In an alternative work, Furfaroa et al. [50] offered a scalable platform, known as SmallWorld, which enables security professionals to design various scenarios to assess vulnerabilities related to IoT devices. By uniquely reproducing the behavior of human users and their corresponding events, the authors created a practical capability to achieve the intended objective. The architecture of their proposed platform is composed of five layers; including physical, abstraction, core service, API, and management layers. Such a composition offers data replication mechanisms, provides a scalable platform, puts forward an API for deploying IoT-tailored simulation scenarios, and facilitates the gathering and analysis of related descriptive statistics. Through variously investigated case studies in the context of home automation applications, the authors illustrated the effectiveness of the platform by permitting formal evaluation of IoT security. The researchers stated that such an approach allows identifying IoT security issues prior to operating such IoT devices in production contexts. Since fuzzy-based approaches similar to [48] are widely applied in traditional IT realms, Lahmadi et al. [74] designed a testing framework that enables developers to assess the security of the 6LoWPAN [126] protocol. By employing mutation algorithms to messages at different network layers, the testing suite analyzes deviations from expected and actual responses of IoT devices. The authors focused on the Contiki 6LoWPAN implementation, leaving other variants for future work. Along the same research direction, Cui et al. [30] applied a fuzzy technique [48] to ZigBee networks to locate and analyze vulnerabilities within IoT networks. The authors combined Finite State Machines (FSM) with a structure-based fuzzy algorithms suited for the MAC protocol of Zigbee. To verify the proposed technique, the researchers conducted a series of performance tests. The results unveiled that compared to random-based algorithms, the proposed FSM-fuzzy framework is more cost-effective, while compared to a structure-based algorithm, its results are more accurate.

2.9.2 Honeypots

Behaving like real IoT assets while having no value for an attacker, honeypots trap and analyze an adversary by intentionally creating security vulnerabilities. These devices (or their software counterparts) capture malicious activities for further investigation of attack vectors or to generate attack patters, which could be used for future mitigation. Honeypots, however, mimic a very specific type of devices in a particular environment, introducing major scalability issue in the context of the IoT ecosystem.

Pa Pa et al. [97] were among the first to pioneer IoT-specific honeypots. The researchers offered a trap-based monitoring system dubbed as IoTPOT, which emulates Telnet services of various IoT devices to analyze ongoing attacks in depth. The authors observed a significant number of attempts to download external malware binary files. The authors distinguished three steps of Telnet-based attacks, namely, intrusion, infection and monetization. During the first phase, the researchers observed numerous login attempts with a fixed or a random order of credentials. The authors distinguished ten main patterns of command sequences which are used to prepare the environment for the next step. In the second stage of an attack, the device downloads the malware, while in the last step, controlled by an attacker, the device conducts DDoS attacks, Telnet and TCP port scans, and spread malware. Moreover, the authors presented IoTBOX, a multi-architecture malware sandbox, that is used for analysis of captured binaries. Consequently, five distinct malware families where discovered. The authors, however, did not provide geo-location information about the sources of the attacks. In alternative work, Guarnizo et al. [60] presented the Scalable high-Interaction Honeypot platform (SIPHON) for IoT devices. The authors demonstrated how by leveraging worldwide wormholes and few physical devices, it is possible to mimic numerous IoT devices on the Internet and to attract malicious traffic. The authors further provided insights regarding such traffic, including the popularity of target locations, scanned ports, and user agents. Similarly, Vasilomanolakis et al. [141] proposed HosTaGe, a honeypot that aims to detect malicious activities targeting ICS networks. HosTaGe supports the identification of attacks in various protocols as HTTP, SMB, Telnet, FTP, MySQL, SIP, and SSH. Upon detection, the proposed honeypot generates effective attack signatures to be employed in IDS for future detection and thus mitigation. In another work, to detect targeted attacks against ICS which rely on Programmable Logic Controllers (PLC), Buza et al. [20] designed the Crysys honeypot. Such honeypot, which was evaluated in a lab environment, was capable to detect port scans and numerous brute-force attempts via SSH. Additionally, Litchfield et al. [79] proposed a CPS framework supporting a hybrid-interaction honeypot architecture. The proposed honeypot known as HoneyPhy aims to provide the ability to simulate the behavior of both CPS processes and IoT devices. The framework consists of three modules; Internet interfaces, process modules, and device models. The first component maintains connections, manages outgoing packets, and alters traffic packets if necessary. The second element correctly emulates the systems' dynamics related to the physical process. Finally, the last component encompasses CPS devices and mimics their logic. The proposed honeypot was instrumented in a lab environment where its capability to simulate real systems was assessed and reported. In alternative work, Dowling et al. [35] designed a honeypot which simulates a ZigBee gateway to explore attacks against ZigBee-based IoT devices. By modifying an existing SSH honeypot, namely Kippo [1], using a set of Python scripts, the authors monitored 3-month activities targeting the Zigbee gateway. The researchers reported six types of executed attacks. These include dictionary and bruteforce attacks, scans, botnets and a number of other independent events. The authors reported that dictionary attacks represented nearly 94% of all attacks.

2.9.3 Network Discovery

Given the large-scale deployment of vulnerable IoT devices, it is essential to have a scalable capacity to identify (vulnerable or compromised) devices at large for prompt remediation. To this end, network discovery techniques become an utmost priority.

In this context, Fachkha et al. [43] recently analyzed attackers' intentions when targeting protocols of Internet-facing CPS. The authors leveraged passive measurements to report on a large number of stealthy scanning activity targeting more than 20 heavily employed CPS protocols. Alternatively, Galluscio el al. [52] illustrated the widespread insecurity of IoT devices by proposing a unique approach to identify unsolicited IoT nodes. By leveraging large darknet (passive) data and applying a correlation algorithm, the authors determined nearly 12,000 attempts to exploit different Internet host generated by compromised IoT devices. The approach supports the inference of such compromised devices in various IoT deployment environments, rendering it possible to leverage the proposed approach for an Internet-scale application. From an industrial perspective, the search engine for Internet-connected devices Shodan [127] crawls the Internet 24/7 and updates its repository in real-time to provide an recent list of IoT devices. By grabbing and analyzing banners and device meta-data, Shodan conducts testing for various vulnerabilities including Heartbleed, Logjam, and default passwords. In a similar manner, the search engine Censys [37] collects data (including IoT information) through executing horizontal scans of the public IPv4 address space and provides public access to raw data through a web service. In contrast, Meidan et al. [85] leveraged network traffic analysis to classify IoT devices connected to an organization's network. By applying single-session classifiers, the authors were able to distinguish IoT devices among other hosts with 99% accuracy. The proposed method holds promise to enable reliable identification of IoT connections in an enterprise setting. Similarly, Formby et al. [47] designed two approaches for device fingerprinting. The first method leverages the cross-layer response time while the second utilizes the unique physical properties of IoT devices. The accuracy of both methods is 99% and 92%, respectively.

2.9.4   Intrusion Detection

An effective approach to infer malicious attempts generated from the IoT paradigm is to employ Intrusion Detection Systems (IDS). Such mechanisms support both detection and prompt response to malicious activities. Given the limited resources of IoT devices, most deployed intrusion detection techniques are network-based with an active response system, which operates by halting communications of the compromised nodes.

Raza et al. [112] pioneered an IDS, known as SVELTE, for IoT contexts. The authors explained how monitoring of inconsistencies in node communications by observing network topology protects IoT devices against various known attacks. The system consists of three centralized modules that are deployed in a 6LoW-PAN Border Router. The first component, namely 6Mapper, gathers information about the network, reconstructs a Destination-Oriented Directed Acyclic Graph

(DODAG), and infuses the node's parent and neighbors information into DODAG. The second module is responsible for analysis and intrusion detection, while the third module acts as a simplistic firewall which filters unwanted traffic before it reaches the resource-constrained network. The proposed approach proved its ability in accurately detecting various malicious misdemeanors. More recently, to enhance the security within 6LoWPAN networks, Shreenivas et al. [128] extended SVELTE with two additional modules. The first is an intrusion detection module that uses Expected Transmissions (ETX) metrics, monitoring of which can prevent an adversary from engaging 6LoWPAN nodes in malicious activities. The second module consists of a technique which attempts to locate malicious nodes inside the 6LoWPAN network. To make these extensions possible, the authors complemented the 6Mapper with an ETX value, making it part of each received request. An intrusion is determined by comparing the parent and children's ETX values; the parent's ETX should be lower than that of its children. In cases where an attacker compromises the node and its neighbors, it is hard for 6Mapper to distinguish the inconsistencies using ETX values. To mitigate this limitation, the authors proposed to utilize the knowledge of node location and cluster the nodes to identify their immediate neighbors. The technique allows the determination of IoT devices with fake identities, thus proactively preventing various attacks. Further, Yang et al. [152] proposed a scheme that enables the detection of FDI attacks in IoT-based environmental surveillance at an early stage. To this end, the authors leveraged state estimation techniques based on Divided Difference Filtering (DDF) to detect false aggregated data and Sequential Hypothesis Testing (SHT) to determine the nodes that are suspected of injecting false data. The detection framework comprises of two modules: (1) local false data detection and (2) malicious aggregate identifier. The first module conducts the threshold-based detection of the data falsification, while the second module utilizes the result of the first one to take further decision. An evaluation of the scheme demonstrated high detection rate with a low false positive rate. In alternative work, Thanigaivelan et al. [137] leveraged collaboration between 1-hop neighbor nodes to design a distributed anomaly detection system for the IoT paradigm. Each node is responsible for monitoring the behavior of its neighbors. In particular, the approach monitors packet size and data rate. Once an anomaly is detected, the abnormally-behaving node is isolated from the network by discarding the packets at the link layer, and the observed event is escalated to a parent node. Further, Parno et al. [99] proposed two distributed schemes, namely, randomized and line-selected multicast, for detecting nodes' replications. The first proposed algorithm is based upon a broadcast protocol in which each node floods the network with its identity and location information. Further, randomly selected nodes collect this data and check whether locations are the same for particular nodes. Two conflicting points would trigger the network to revoke a node. This algorithm assumes that each node is aware of its position and network by employing an identity-based public key system. The second proposed algorithm eliminates the step where each node broadcast its location within the network but instead shares it with randomly selected nodes directly. If a node that is responsible for detection receives two different locations for the same identity, it triggers a network response to revoke that node. The authors evaluated both algorithms in a lab environment and confirmed that the second method requires fewer communication packets, while the first method provides higher resiliency since it prevents an adversary from anticipating the node which is responsible for detection. In another work, Bostani et al. [17] proposed a novel real-time intrusion detection framework for detecting malicious behaviors against routing protocols within an IoT network. In particular, the authors investigated sinkhole and selective-forwarding attacks. Both router and root nodes participate in the detection decision making. Analysis begins with the router node, which applies specification-based detection mechanisms to its host nodes and sends the results to the root node. In turns, a detection mechanism employed at the root node employs the unsupervised optimum-path forest algorithm for projecting clustering models using the incoming data packets. The results of both analysis are leveraged as input to the voting mechanism for intrusion detection. Alternatively, aiming to reduce energy depletion in a wireless sensor network, Patel and Soni [100] proposed to keep the energy level of a node in a routing table. Further, the communication protocol calculates the threshold energy $(Th(E))$ and compare it with the energy level (EN_i) of the next node. In case $EN_i > Th(E)$ a communication packet is sent, otherwise, the protocol employs the procedure of route repairment. In an different work, Midi et al. [88] proposed a self-adaptive knowledge-driven IDS, namely Kalis, that is capable of detecting attacks against IoT environments across a wide range of protocols. Kali could be implemented as a smart firewall to filter suspicious incoming traffic from the Internet. By observing the available events and determining features of entities and networks, the system determines which detection technique to activate to infer a security incident. By keeping in mind the heterogeneous nature of IoT devices, communication protocols, and software, the authors designed the system, so that it does not require software alterations, complies with various communication standards, is extensible to new technologies, and avoids significant performance overhead. Moreover, the proposed system enables knowledge sharing and collaborative detection techniques. System evaluation demonstrated the accuracy of the approach in detecting various attacks. Additional, Yu et al. [154] argued that traditional host-based solutions are not applicable in IoT realms due to device constraints and their deployment in various environments. To overcome such limitations, the authors specified three dimensions through which the network traffic related to IoT has to be subjected. These include an environmental and security-relevant contexts along with cross-device interactions. The authors proposed a crowd-sourced repository for sharing and exchanging attack signatures. Finally, the researchers suggested a security enforcement technique, which extends Software-Defined Networks (SDNs) and Network Functions Virtualization (NFV) to the IoT context and employs the concept of micro-middleboxes for real-time remediation of vulnerable IoT devices.

To contribute to the objective of detecting IoT maliciousness, several research attempts have been made on large-scale vulnerability notifications. Nonetheless, a plethora of them center on compromised websites hosting IoT devices [77, 133], while only one investigated the effectiveness of IoT situational awareness. To this end, Li et al. [76] demonstrated how message content and contact point affect

Table 2.8 IoT security situational awareness capabilities

Vulnerability	Situational awareness capability[a]				References
	V	H	N	I	
Deficient physical security	✓			✓	[98, 112]
Insufficient energy harvesting				✓	[17, 99, 111, 127]
Inadequate authentication	✓		✓	✓	[7, 15, 50, 87, 98, 111, 128, 151]
Improper encryption	✓				[30, 73, 128]
Unnecessarily open ports	✓	✓			[20, 59, 78, 96, 128, 134, 140]
Insufficient access control	✓	✓	✓		[18, 20, 35, 37, 43, 51, 52, 59, 78, 96, 126, 128, 134, 140]
Improper patch management capabilities	✓				[134]
Weak programming practices	✓			✓	[50, 87, 111, 128, 134, 151]
Insufficient audit mechanism				✓	[87, 111, 151]
Compromised device identification			✓	✓	[17, 17, 51, 87, 92, 98, 99, 111, 125, 127, 135, 136, 151]

[a] *V* Vulnerability Assessment, *H* Honeypots, *N* Network Discovery, *I* Intrusion Detection

fix rate of vulnerabilities for ICS. In particular, the results indicate that the most effective method is direct notification with detailed information. However, the authors pinpointed that the majority of contacts did not respond or fixed their problem. Thus, the effectiveness of such notification remains an open question and undoubtedly requires attention from the security research and operational communities.

The relationship between the available situational awareness capabilities in addressing the pinpointed IoT vulnerabilities is summarized and illustrated in Table 2.8.

Findings

Many techniques already exist that aim at identifying IoT security weaknesses, learning attackers' behaviors and continuously monitoring devices for proper remediation. Nevertheless, the status of their practical implementation in IoT contexts remains somehow ambiguous. Further, many approaches do not seem to be generic enough to address the heterogeneity of IoT paradigm. Additionally, while we note that intrusion detection techniques in IoT realms demonstrate advanced progress, some of their methodologies leave the room for further research. Indeed, relying only on IDS mechanisms in an attempt to monitor intrusions seems to be not very effective, since they only detect limited attacks as illustrated in Table 2.9.

Table 2.9 Intrusion detection techniques deployed in IoT environments

Author	Dictionary attack	Side-channel attack	Sybil attack	False data injection	Firmware modifica-tion	Device capturing	Sinkhole attack	Battery draining attack	Selective-forwarding	Anomaly detection
Behavior-based										
Raza et al. [111]			✓	✓			✓		✓	
Shreenivas et al. [127]								✓	✓	
Yang et al. [151]				✓						
Thanigaivelan et al. [136]										✓
Parno et al. [98]						✓				
Knowledge-based										
Bostani et al. [17]							✓		✓	
Patel and Soni [99]								✓		
Midi et al. [87]				✓					✓	

Nevertheless, passive data-driven approaches hold promise to overcome these limitations, while, in general, the probability of inferring exploited devices remains obscure and requires further investigation.

References

1. Kippo - ssh honeypot. https://github.com/desaster/kippo.
2. Payatu. IoT security – part 3 (101 – IoT top ten vulnerabilities). https://payatu.com/iot-security-part-3-101-iot-top-ten-vulnerabilities/.
3. Ala Al-Fuqaha, Mohsen Guizani, Mehdi Mohammadi, Mohammed Aledhari, and Moussa Ayyash. Internet of things: A survey on enabling technologies, protocols, and applications. *IEEE Communications Surveys & Tutorials*, 17(4):2347–2376, 2015.
4. Fadele Ayotunde Alaba, Mazliza Othman, Ibrahim Abaker Targio Hashem, and Faiz Alotaibi. Internet of things security: A survey. *Journal of Network and Computer Applications*, 2017.
5. Andres Riancho. w3af - open source web application security scanner. www.w3af.org.
6. Kishore Angrishi. Turning internet of things (IoT) into internet of vulnerabilities (IoV): Iot botnets. *arXiv preprint arXiv:1702.03681*, 2017.
7. Anonymous. Internet census 2012: Port scanning/0 using insecure embedded devices. *URL* http://internetcensus2012.bitbucket.org/paper.html, 2012.
8. Manos Antonakakis, Tim April, Michael Bailey, Matt Bernhard, Elie Bursztein, Jaime Cochran, Zakir Durumeric, J Alex Halderman, Luca Invernizzi, Michalis Kallitsis, et al. Understanding the Mirai botnet. In *26th {USENIX} Security Symposium ({USENIX} Security 17)*, pages 1093–1110, 2017.
9. Luigi Atzori, Antonio Iera, and Giacomo Morabito. The internet of things: A survey. *Computer networks*, 54(15):2787–2805, 2010.
10. Luigi Atzori, Antonio Iera, and Giacomo Morabito. Understanding the internet of things: definition, potentials, and societal role of a fast evolving paradigm. *Ad Hoc Networks*, 2016.
11. Tuomas Aura. Cryptographically generated addresses (CGA). https://www.rfc-editor.org/info/rfc3972, 2005.
12. V Balasubramanian, Nikolaos Kouvelas, K Chandra, RV Prasad, Artemios G Voyiatzis, and W Liu. A unified architecture for integrating energy harvesting iot devices with the mobile edge cloud. In *2018 IEEE 4th World Forum on Internet of Things (WF-IoT)*, pages 13–18. IEEE, 2018.
13. Zachry Basnight, Jonathan Butts, Juan Lopez, and Thomas Dube. Firmware modification attacks on programmable logic controllers. *International Journal of Critical Infrastructure Protection*, 6(2):76–84, 2013.
14. Boldizsár Bencsáth, Levente Buttyán, and Tamás Paulik. Xcs based hidden firmware modification on embedded devices. In *Software, Telecommunications and Computer Networks (SoftCOM), 2011 19th International Conference on*, pages 1–5. IEEE, 2011.
15. Alex Biryukov, Daniel Dinu, and Yann Le Corre. Side-channel attacks meet secure network protocols. In *International Conference on Applied Cryptography and Network Security*, pages 435–454. Springer, 2017.
16. Tamara Bonaci, Linda Bushnell, and Radha Poovendran. Node capture attacks in wireless sensor networks: A system theoretic approach. In *Decision and Control (CDC), 2010 49th IEEE Conference on*, pages 6765–6772. IEEE, 2010.
17. Hamid Bostani and Mansour Sheikhan. Hybrid of anomaly-based and specification-based IDS for internet of things using unsupervised OPF based on mapreduce approach. *Computer Communications*, 98:52–71, 2017.

18. Elias Bou-Harb, Walter Lucia, Nicola Forti, Sean Weerakkody, Nasir Ghani, and Bruno Sinopoli. Cyber meets control: A novel federated approach for resilient cps leveraging real cyber threat intelligence. *IEEE Communications Magazine*, 55(5):198–204, 2017.
19. BullGuard. http://www.dojo-labs.com/.
20. Dániel István Buza, Ferenc Juhász, György Miru, Márk Félegyházi, and Tamás Holczer. Cryplh: Protecting smart energy systems from targeted attacks with a PLC honeypot. In *International Workshop on Smart Grid Security*, pages 181–192. Springer, 2014.
21. M Campagna. Sec 4: Elliptic curve Qu-Vanstone implicit certificate scheme (ECQV). *vol*, 4:32, 2013.
22. Cisco. The internet of things reference model. [Online]. Available: https://www.cisco.com/c/dam/global/en_ph/.../jim_green_cisco_connect.pdf. Accessed 2018-03-05.
23. Bogdan Copos, Karl Levitt, Matt Bishop, and Jeff Rowe. Is anybody home? inferring activity from smart home network traffic. In *Security and Privacy Workshops (SPW), 2016 IEEE*, pages 245–251. IEEE, 2016.
24. Daniel G Costa, Ivanovitch Silva, Luiz Affonso Guedes, Francisco Vasques, and Paulo Portugal. Availability issues in wireless visual sensor networks. *Sensors*, 14(2):2795–2821, 2014.
25. Andrei Costin, Jonas Zaddach, Aurélien Francillon, Davide Balzarotti, and Sophia Antipolis. A large-scale analysis of the security of embedded firmwares. In *USENIX Security*, pages 95–110, 2014.
26. Andrei Costin, Apostolis Zarras, and Aurélien Francillon. Automated dynamic firmware analysis at scale: a case study on embedded web interfaces. In *Proceedings of the 11th ACM on Asia Conference on Computer and Communications Security*, pages 437–448. ACM, 2016.
27. CRIMESIDER STAFF, CBS news. Baby monitor hacker delivers creepy message to child. https://www.cbsnews.com/news/baby-monitor-hacker-delivers-creepy-message-to-child/.
28. Ang Cui, Michael Costello, and Salvatore J Stolfo. When firmware modifications attack: A case study of embedded exploitation. In *NDSS*, 2013.
29. Ang Cui and Salvatore J Stolfo. A quantitative analysis of the insecurity of embedded network devices: results of a wide-area scan. In *Proceedings of the 26th Annual Computer Security Applications Conference*, pages 97–106. ACM, 2010.
30. Baojiang Cui, Shurui Liang, Shilei Chen, Bing Zhao, and Xiaobing Liang. A novel fuzzing method for Zigbee based on finite state machine. *International Journal of Distributed Sensor Networks*, 10(1):762891, 2014.
31. CUJO. https://www.getcujo.com/.
32. Jakub Czyz, Matthew J Luckie, Mark Allman, and Michael Bailey. Don't forget to lock the back door! a characterization of ipv6 network security policy. In *NDSS*, 2016.
33. Li Da Xu, Wu He, and Shancang Li. Internet of things in industries: A survey. *IEEE Transactions on Industrial Informatics*, 10(4):2233–2243, 2014.
34. Parwinder Kaur Dhillon and Sheetal Kalra. A lightweight biometrics based remote user authentication scheme for iot services. *Journal of Information Security and Applications*, 2017.
35. Seamus Dowling, Michael Schukat, and Hugh Melvin. A Zigbee honeypot to assess iot cyberattack behaviour. In *Signals and Systems Conference (ISSC), 2017 28th Irish*, pages 1–6. IEEE, 2017.
36. Adam Dunkels, Oliver Schmidt, Niclas Finne, Joakim Eriksson, Fredrik Österlind, Nicolas Tsiftes, and Mathilde Durvy. The Contiki OS: The operating system for the internet of things. *Online], at* http://www.contikios.org, 2011.
37. Zakir Durumeric, David Adrian, Ariana Mirian, Michael Bailey, and J Alex Halderman. A search engine backed by internet-wide scanning. In *Proceedings of the 22nd ACM SIGSAC Conference on Computer and Communications Security*, pages 542–553. ACM, 2015.
38. Zakir Durumeric, James Kasten, Michael Bailey, and J Alex Halderman. Analysis of the https certificate ecosystem. In *Proceedings of the 2013 conference on Internet measurement conference*, pages 291–304. ACM, 2013.

39. Ata Elahi and Adam Gschwender. *ZigBee wireless sensor and control network*. Pearson Education, 2009.
40. Haytham Elmiligi, Fayez Gebali, and M Watheq El-Kharashi. Multi-dimensional analysis of embedded systems security. *Microprocessors and Microsystems*, 41:29–36, 2016.
41. Hewlett Packard Enterprise. Internet of things research study. *Internet of Things Research Study*, 2015.
42. Laurent Eschenauer and Virgil D Gligor. A key-management scheme for distributed sensor networks. In *Proceedings of the 9th ACM Conference on Computer and Communications Security*, pages 41–47. ACM, 2002.
43. Claude Fachkha, Elias Bou-Harb, Anastasis Keliris, Nasir Memon, and Mustaque Ahamad. Internet-scale probing of cps: Inference, characterization and orchestration analysis. In *Proceedings of NDSS*, volume 17, 2017.
44. Shahin Farahani. *ZigBee wireless networks and transceivers*. newnes, 2011.
45. Qian Feng, Rundong Zhou, Chengcheng Xu, Yao Cheng, Brian Testa, and Heng Yin. Scalable graph-based bug search for firmware images. In *Proceedings of the 2016 ACM SIGSAC Conference on Computer and Communications Security*, pages 480–491. ACM, 2016.
46. Earlence Fernandes, Justin Paupore, Amir Rahmati, Daniel Simionato, Mauro Conti, and Atul Prakash. Flowfence: Practical data protection for emerging iot application frameworks. In *USENIX Security Symposium*, 2016.
47. David Formby, Preethi Srinivasan, Andrew Leonard, Jonathan Rogers, and Raheem Beyah. Who's in control of your control system? device fingerprinting for cyber-physical systems. In *Network and Distributed System Security Symposium (NDSS)*, 2016.
48. Justin E Forrester and Barton P Miller. An empirical study of the robustness of windows NT applications using random testing. In *Proceedings of the 4th USENIX Windows System Symposium*, pages 59–68. Seattle, 2000.
49. Lorenzo Franceschi-Bicchierai. Internet of things teddy bear leaked 2 million parent and kids message recordings, Feb 2017.
50. Angelo Furfaro, Luciano Argento, Andrea Parise, and Antonio Piccolo. Using virtual environments for the assessment of cybersecurity issues in iot scenarios. *Simulation Modelling Practice and Theory*, 73:43–54, 2017.
51. Nataliia Neshenko, Elias Bou-Harb, Jorge Crichigno, Georges Kaddoum, and Nasir Ghani. Demystifying IoT Security: an Exhaustive Survey on IoT Vulnerabilities and a First Empirical Look on Internet-scale IoT Exploitations. *IEEE Communications Surveys & Tutorials*, 2019.
52. M. Galluscio, N. Neshenko, E. Bou-Harb, Y. Huang, N. Ghani, J. Crichigno, and G. Kaddoum. A first empirical look on internet-scale exploitations of iot devices. In *2017 IEEE 28th Annual International Symposium on Personal, Indoor, and Mobile Radio Communications (PIMRC)*, pages 1–7, Oct 2017.
53. Usha Devi Gandhi, Priyan Malarvizhi Kumar, R Varatharajan, Gunasekaran Manogaran, Revathi Sundarasekar, and Shreyas Kadu. Hiotpot: surveillance on iot devices against recent threats. *Wireless personal communications*, pages 1–16, 2018.
54. Oscar Garcia-Morchon, Sye Loong Keoh, Sandeep Kumar, Pedro Moreno-Sanchez, Francisco Vidal-Meca, and Jan Henrik Ziegeldorf. Securing the IP-based internet of things with HIP and DTLS. In *Proceedings of the sixth ACM conference on Security and privacy in wireless and mobile networks*, pages 119–124. ACM, 2013.
55. Audrey A Gendreau and Michael Moorman. Survey of intrusion detection systems towards an end to end secure internet of things. In *Future Internet of Things and Cloud (FiCloud), 2016 IEEE 4th International Conference on*, pages 84–90. IEEE, 2016.
56. K. Georgiou, S. Xavier de Souza, and K. Eder. The iot energy challenge: A software perspective. *IEEE Embedded Systems Letters*, 10(3):53–56, Sep. 2018.
57. Branden Ghena, William Beyer, Allen Hillaker, Jonathan Pevarnek, and J Alex Halderman. Green lights forever: Analyzing the security of traffic infrastructure. *WOOT*, 14:7–7, 2014.
58. Ghada Glissa and Aref Meddeb. 6lowpan multi-layered security protocol based on IEEE 802.15. 4 security features. In *Wireless Communications and Mobile Computing Conference (IWCMC), 2017 13th International*, pages 264–269. IEEE, 2017.

59. Jorge Granjal, Edmundo Monteiro, and Jorge Sá Silva. Security for the internet of things: a survey of existing protocols and open research issues. *IEEE Communications Surveys & Tutorials*, 17(3):1294–1312, 2015.

60. Juan Guarnizo, Amit Tambe, Suman Sankar Bunia, Martín Ochoa, Nils Tippenhauer, Asaf Shabtai, and Yuval Elovici. Siphon: Towards scalable high-interaction physical honeypots. *arXiv preprint arXiv:1701.02446*, 2017.

61. Jayavardhana Gubbi, Rajkumar Buyya, Slaven Marusic, and Marimuthu Palaniswami. Internet of things (iot): A vision, architectural elements, and future directions. *Future generation computer systems*, 29(7):1645–1660, 2013.

62. Zimu Guo, Nima Karimian, Mark M Tehranipoor, and Domenic Forte. Hardware security meets biometrics for the age of iot. In *Circuits and Systems (ISCAS), 2016 IEEE International Symposium on*, pages 1318–1321. IEEE, 2016.

63. Ibbad Hafeez, Aaron Yi Ding, Lauri Suomalainen, Alexey Kirichenko, and Sasu Tarkoma. Securebox: Toward safer and smarter iot networks. In *Proceedings of the 2016 ACM Workshop on Cloud-Assisted Networking*, pages 55–60. ACM, 2016.

64. Xiali Hei, Xiaojiang Du, Jie Wu, and Fei Hu. Defending resource depletion attacks on implantable medical devices. In *Global Telecommunications Conference (GLOBECOM 2010), 2010 IEEE*, pages 1–5. IEEE, 2010.

65. Grant Ho, Derek Leung, Pratyush Mishra, Ashkan Hosseini, Dawn Song, and David Wagner. Smart locks: Lessons for securing commodity internet of things devices. In *Proceedings of the 11th ACM on Asia Conference on Computer and Communications Security*, pages 461–472. ACM, 2016.

66. M Shamim Hossain, Ghulam Muhammad, Sk Md Mizanur Rahman, Wadood Abdul, Abdulhameed Alelaiwi, and Atif Alamri. Toward end-to-end biometrics-based security for iot infrastructure. *IEEE Wireless Communications*, 23(5):44–51, 2016.

67. Inc IoT Defense. Rattrap. https://www.myrattrap.com/.

68. Mian Ahmad Jan, Priyadarsi Nanda, Xiangjian He, Zhiyuan Tan, and Ren Ping Liu. A robust authentication scheme for observing resources in the internet of things environment. In *Trust, Security and Privacy in Computing and Communications (TrustCom), 2014 IEEE 13th International Conference on*, pages 205–211. IEEE, 2014.

69. Yunhan Jack Jia, Qi Alfred Chen, Shiqi Wang, Amir Rahmati, Earlence Fernandes, Zhuoqing Morley Mao, Atul Prakash, and Shanghai JiaoTong University. Contexlot: Towards providing contextual integrity to appified IoT platforms. In *NDSS*, 2017.

70. P. Kamalinejad, C. Mahapatra, Z. Sheng, S. Mirabbasi, V. C. M. Leung, and Y. L. Guan. Wireless energy harvesting for the internet of things. *IEEE Communications Magazine*, 53(6):102–108, June 2015.

71. Constantinos Kolias, Georgios Kambourakis, Angelos Stavrou, and Jeffrey Voas. Ddos in the iot: Mirai and other botnets. *Computer*, 50(7):80–84, 2017.

72. C. Konstantinou and M. Maniatakos. Impact of firmware modification attacks on power systems field devices. In *2015 IEEE International Conference on Smart Grid Communications (SmartGridComm)*, pages 283–288, Nov 2015.

73. Thomas Kothmayr, Corinna Schmitt, Wen Hu, Michael Brünig, and Georg Carle. Dtls based security and two-way authentication for the internet of things. *Ad Hoc Networks*, 11(8):2710–2723, 2013.

74. Abdelkader Lahmadi, Cesar Brandin, and Olivier Festor. A testing framework for discovering vulnerabilities in 6lowpan networks. In *Distributed Computing in Sensor Systems (DCOSS), 2012 IEEE 8th International Conference on*, pages 335–340. IEEE, 2012.

75. Chunxiao Li, Anand Raghunathan, and Niraj K Jha. Improving the trustworthiness of medical device software with formal verification methods. *IEEE Embedded Systems Letters*, 5(3):50–53, 2013.

76. Frank Li, Zakir Durumeric, Jakub Czyz, Mohammad Karami, Michael Bailey, Damon McCoy, Stefan Savage, and Vern Paxson. You've got vulnerability: Exploring effective vulnerability notifications. In *USENIX Security Symposium (Aug. 2016)*, 2016.

77. Frank Li, Grant Ho, Eric Kuan, Yuan Niu, Lucas Ballard, Kurt Thomas, Elie Bursztein, and Vern Paxson. Remedying web hijacking: Notification effectiveness and webmaster comprehension. In *Proceedings of the 25th International Conference on World Wide Web*, pages 1009–1019. International World Wide Web Conferences Steering Committee, 2016.
78. Gaoqi Liang, Junhua Zhao, Fengji Luo, Steven Weller, and Zhao Yang Dong. A review of false data injection attacks against modern power systems. *IEEE Transactions on Smart Grid*, 2017.
79. Samuel Litchfield, David Formby, Jonathan Rogers, Sakis Meliopoulos, and Raheem Beyah. Rethinking the honeypot for cyber-physical systems. *IEEE Internet Computing*, 20(5):9–17, 2016.
80. Xuan Liu, Zhen Bao, Dan Lu, and Zuyi Li. Modeling of local false data injection attacks with reduced network information. *IEEE Transactions on Smart Grid*, 6(4):1686–1696, 2015.
81. Yao Liu, Peng Ning, and Michael K Reiter. False data injection attacks against state estimation in electric power grids. *ACM Transactions on Information and System Security (TISSEC)*, 14(1):13, 2011.
82. Luma. https://lumahome.com/.
83. Rwan Mahmoud, Tasneem Yousuf, Fadi Aloul, and Imn Zualkernan. Internet of things (iot) security: Current status, challenges and prospective measures. In *2015 10th International Conference for Internet Technology and Secured Transactions (ICITST)*, pages 336–341. IEEE, 2015.
84. Linda Markowsky and George Markowsky. Scanning for vulnerable devices in the internet of things. In *Intelligent Data Acquisition and Advanced Computing Systems: Technology and Applications (IDAACS), 2015 IEEE 8th International Conference on*, volume 1, pages 463–467. IEEE, 2015.
85. Yair Meidan, Michael Bohadana, Asaf Shabtai, Juan David Guarnizo, Martín Ochoa, Nils Ole Tippenhauer, and Yuval Elovici. Profiliot: a machine learning approach for iot device identification based on network traffic analysis. In *Proceedings of the symposium on applied computing*, pages 506–509. ACM, 2017.
86. Carnegie Mellon. Cbmc. bounded model checking for software. http://www.cprover.org/cbmc/.
87. Metropolitan.fi. Ddos attack halts heating in finland amidst winter. https://metropolitan.fi/entry/ddos-attack-halts-heating-in-finland-amidst-winter.
88. Daniele Midi, Antonino Rullo, Anand Mudgerikar, and Elisa Bertino. Kalis—a system for knowledge-driven adaptable intrusion detection for the internet of things. In *Distributed Computing Systems (ICDCS), 2017 IEEE 37th International Conference on*, pages 656–666. IEEE, 2017.
89. Andreas F Molisch, Kannan Balakrishnan, Chia-Chin Chong, Shahriar Emami, Andrew Fort, Johan Karedal, Juergen Kunisch, Hans Schantz, Ulrich Schuster, and Kai Siwiak. Ieee 802.15. 4a channel model-final report. *IEEE P802*, 15(04):0662, 2004.
90. Philipp Morgner, Stephan Mattejat, and Zinaida Benenson. All your bulbs are belong to us: Investigating the current state of security in connected lighting systems. *arXiv preprint arXiv:1608.03732*, 2016.
91. A. Mosenia and N. K. Jha. A comprehensive study of security of internet-of-things. *IEEE Transactions on Emerging Topics in Computing*, 5(4):586–602, Oct 2017.
92. R Moskowitz, T Heer, P Jokela, and T Henderson. Host identity protocol version 2 (hipv2), 2015.
93. Fredrik Osterlind. A sensor network simulator for the Contiki OS. *Swedish Institute of Computer Science (SICS), Tech. Rep. T2006-05*, 2006.
94. Aafaf Ouaddah, Hajar Mousannif, Anas Abou Elkalam, and Abdellah Ait Ouahman. Access control in the internet of things: Big challenges and new opportunities. *Computer Networks*, 112:237–262, 2017.
95. OWASP. Owasp zed attack proxy project. [Online]. Available: https://www.owasp.org/index.php/OWASP_Zed_Attack_Proxy_Project. Accessed 2018-03-05.

96. Colin O'Flynn and Zhizhang Chen. Power analysis attacks against ieee 802.15. 4 nodes. In *International Workshop on Constructive Side-Channel Analysis and Secure Design*, pages 55–70. Springer, 2016.
97. Yin Minn Pa Pa, Shogo Suzuki, Katsunari Yoshioka, Tsutomu Matsumoto, Takahiro Kasama, and Christian Rossow. Iotpot: A novel honeypot for revealing current iot threats. *Journal of Information Processing*, 24(3):522–533, 2016.
98. Chang-Seop Park. A secure and efficient ecqv implicit certificate issuance protocol for the internet of things applications. *IEEE Sensors Journal*, 2016.
99. Bryan Parno, Adrian Perrig, and Virgil Gligor. Distributed detection of node replication attacks in sensor networks. In *Security and Privacy, 2005 IEEE Symposium on*, pages 49–63. IEEE, 2005.
100. Amee A Patel and Sunil J Soni. A novel proposal for defending against vampire attack in WSN. In *Communication Systems and Network Technologies (CSNT), 2015 Fifth International Conference on*, pages 624–627. IEEE, 2015.
101. Mark Patton, Eric Gross, Ryan Chinn, Samantha Forbis, Leon Walker, and Hsinchun Chen. Uninvited connections: a study of vulnerable devices on the internet of things (iot). In *Intelligence and Security Informatics Conference (JISIC), 2014 IEEE Joint*, pages 232–235. IEEE, 2014.
102. Charith Perera, Arkady Zaslavsky, Peter Christen, and Dimitrios Georgakopoulos. Context aware computing for the internet of things: A survey. *IEEE Communications Surveys & Tutorials*, 16(1):414–454, 2014.
103. Nikolaos E Petroulakis, Elias Z Tragos, Alexandros G Fragkiadakis, and George Spanoudakis. A lightweight framework for secure life-logging in smart environments. *Information Security Technical Report*, 17(3):58–70, 2013.
104. C. Pielli, F. Chiariotti, N. Laurenti, A. Zanella, and M. Zorzi. A game-theoretic analysis of energy-depleting jamming attacks. In *2017 International Conference on Computing, Networking and Communications (ICNC)*, pages 100–104, Jan 2017.
105. Pawani Porambage, Corinna Schmitt, Pardeep Kumar, Andrei Gurtov, and Mika Ylianttila. Pauthkey: A pervasive authentication protocol and key establishment scheme for wireless sensor networks in distributed iot applications. *International Journal of Distributed Sensor Networks*, 2014.
106. Open Web Application Security Project. Top 10 iot vulnerabilities (2014). [Online]. Available: https://www.owasp.org/index.php/Top_IoT_Vulnerabilities. Accessed 2018-03-05.
107. Mumtaz Qabulio, Yasir Arfat Malkani, and Ayaz Keerio. A framework for securing mobile wireless sensor networks against physical attacks. In *Emerging Technologies (ICET), 2016 International Conference on*, pages 1–6. IEEE, 2016.
108. Pedram Radmand, Marc Domingo, Jaipal Singh, Joan Arnedo, Alex Talevski, Stig Petersen, and Simon Carlsen. Zigbee/Zigbee pro security assessment based on compromised cryptographic keys. In *P2P, Parallel, Grid, Cloud and Internet Computing (3PGCIC), 2010 International Conference on*, pages 465–470. IEEE, 2010.
109. Radware Ltd. "brickerbot" results in PDoS attack. https://security.radware.com/ddos-threats-attacks/brickerbot-pdos-permanent-denial-of-service/.
110. A. Rajan, J. Jithish, and S. Sankaran. Sybil attack in iot: Modelling and defenses. In *2017 International Conference on Advances in Computing, Communications and Informatics (ICACCI)*, pages 2323–2327, Sept 2017.
111. Varshanth R Rao and Anil Kumar KM. Predictive node expiration based energy-aware source routing (PNEB ESR) protocol for wireless sensor networks. In *Proceedings of the 7th ACM India Computing Conference*, page 14. ACM, 2014.
112. Shahid Raza, Linus Wallgren, and Thiemo Voigt. Svelte: Real-time intrusion detection in the internet of things. *Ad hoc networks*, 11(8):2661–2674, 2013.
113. Bradley Reaves and Thomas Morris. An open virtual testbed for industrial control system security research. *International Journal of Information Security*, 11(4):215–229, 2012.
114. Eric Rescorla and Nagendra Modadugu. Datagram transport layer security version 1.2, 2012.

115. Rodrigo Roman, Cristina Alcaraz, Javier Lopez, and Nicolas Sklavos. Key management systems for sensor networks in the context of the internet of things. *Computers & Electrical Engineering*, 37(2):147–159, 2011.
116. Rodrigo Roman, Jianying Zhou, and Javier Lopez. On the features and challenges of security and privacy in distributed internet of things. *Computer Networks*, 57(10):2266–2279, 2013.
117. Eyal Ronen and Adi Shamir. Extended functionality attacks on iot devices: The case of smart lights. In *Security and Privacy (EuroS&P), 2016 IEEE European Symposium on*, pages 3–12. IEEE, 2016.
118. Masoud Rostami, Ari Juels, and Farinaz Koushanfar. Heart-to-heart (h2h): authentication for implanted medical devices. In *Proceedings of the 2013 ACM SIGSAC conference on Computer & communications security*, pages 1099–1112. ACM, 2013.
119. Vinay Sachidananda, Shachar Siboni, Asaf Shabtai, Jinghui Toh, Suhas Bhairav, and Yuval Elovici. Let the cat out of the bag: A holistic approach towards security analysis of the internet of things. In *Proceedings of the 3rd ACM International Workshop on IoT Privacy, Trust, and Security*, pages 3–10. ACM, 2017.
120. Sarosys LLC. Arachni. web application security scanner framework. http://www.arachni-scanner.com/.
121. Augustin P Sarr, Philippe Elbaz-Vincent, and Jean-Claude Bajard. A new security model for authenticated key agreement. In *International Conference on Security and Cryptography for Networks*, pages 219–234. Springer, 2010.
122. Carl Schuett, Jonathan Butts, and Stephen Dunlap. An evaluation of modification attacks on programmable logic controllers. *International Journal of Critical Infrastructure Protection*, 7(1):61–68, 2014.
123. Savio Sciancalepore, Angelo Capossele, Giuseppe Piro, Gennaro Boggia, and Giuseppe Bianchi. Key management protocol with implicit certificates for iot systems. In *Proceedings of the 2015 Workshop on IoT challenges in Mobile and Industrial Systems*, pages 37–42. ACM, 2015.
124. Hossein Shafagh, Anwar Hithnawi, Lukas Burkhalter, Pascal Fischli, and Simon Duquennoy. Secure sharing of partially homomorphic encrypted iot data. In *Proceedings of the 15th ACM Conference on Embedded Network Sensor System*. ACM, 2017.
125. Hossein Shafagh, Anwar Hithnawi, Andreas Dröscher, Simon Duquennoy, and Wen Hu. Talos: Encrypted query processing for the internet of things. In *Proceedings of the 13th ACM Conference on Embedded Networked Sensor Systems*, pages 197–210. ACM, 2015.
126. Zach Shelby and Carsten Bormann. *6LoWPAN: The wireless embedded Internet*, volume 43. John Wiley & Sons, 2011.
127. Shodan®. http://shodan.io.
128. Dharmini Shreenivas, Shahid Raza, and Thiemo Voigt. Intrusion detection in the RPL-connected 6lowpan networks. In *Proceedings of the 3rd ACM International Workshop on IoT Privacy, Trust, and Security*, pages 31–38. ACM, 2017.
129. Shachar Siboni, Asaf Shabtai, Nils O Tippenhauer, Jemin Lee, and Yuval Elovici. Advanced security testbed framework for wearable iot devices. *ACM Transactions on Internet Technology (TOIT)*, 16(4):26, 2016.
130. Sabrina Sicari, Alessandra Rizzardi, Luigi Alfredo Grieco, and Alberto Coen-Porisini. Security, privacy and trust in internet of things: The road ahead. *Computer Networks*, 76:146–164, 2015.
131. Marcos A Simplicio Jr, Marcos VM Silva, Renan CA Alves, and Tiago KC Shibata. Lightweight and escrow-less authenticated key agreement for the internet of things. *Computer Communications*, 2016.
132. Meriem Smache, Nadia El Mrabet, Jesus-Javier Gilquijano, Assia Tria, Emmanuel Riou, and Chaput Gregory. Modeling a node capture attack in a secure wireless sensor networks. In *Internet of Things (WF-IoT), 2016 IEEE 3rd World Forum on*, pages 188–193. IEEE, 2016.
133. Ben Stock, Giancarlo Pellegrino, Christian Rossow, Martin Johns, and Michael Backes. Hey, you have a problem: On the feasibility of large-scale web vulnerability notification. In *USENIX Security Symposium (Aug. 2016)*, 2016.

134. Ali Tekeoglu and Ali Saman Tosun. Investigating security and privacy of a cloud-based wireless ip camera: Netcam. In *Computer Communication and Networks (ICCCN), 2015 24th International Conference on*, pages 1–6. IEEE, 2015.

135. Ali Tekeoglu and Ali Şaman Tosun. A testbed for security and privacy analysis of iot devices. In *Mobile Ad Hoc and Sensor Systems (MASS), 2016 IEEE 13th International Conference on*, pages 343–348. IEEE, 2016.

136. V. Thangavelu, D. M. Divakaran, R. Sairam, S. S. Bhunia, and M. Gurusamy. Deft: A distributed iot fingerprinting technique. *IEEE Internet of Things Journal*, pages 1–1, 2018.

137. Nanda Kumar Thanigaivelan, Ethiopia Nigussie, Rajeev Kumar Kanth, Seppo Virtanen, and Jouni Isoaho. Distributed internal anomaly detection system for internet-of-things. In *Consumer Communications & Networking Conference (CCNC), 2016 13th IEEE Annual*, pages 319–320. IEEE, 2016.

138. Wade Trappe, Richard Howard, and Robert S Moore. Low-energy security: Limits and opportunities in the internet of things. *IEEE Security & Privacy*, 13(1):14–21, 2015.

139. Blase Ur, Jaeyeon Jung, and Stuart Schechter. The current state of access control for smart devices in homes. In *Workshop on Home Usable Privacy and Security (HUPS)*. HUPS 2014, 2013.

140. U.S. Department of Homeland Security. Brickerbot permanent denial-of-service attack (update a). https://ics-cert.us-cert.gov/alerts/ICS-ALERT-17-102-01A.

141. Emmanouil Vasilomanolakis, Shreyas Srinivasa, Carlos Garcia Cordero, and Max Mühlhäuser. Multi-stage attack detection and signature generation with ICS honeypots. In *IEEE/IFIP Workshop on Security for Emerging Distributed Network Technologies (DIS-SECT)*. IEEE, 2016.

142. Eugene Y Vasserman and Nicholas Hopper. Vampire attacks: draining life from wireless ad hoc sensor networks. *IEEE transactions on mobile computing*, 12(2):318–332, 2013.

143. Niko Vidgren, Keijo Haataja, Jose Luis Patino-Andres, Juan Jose Ramirez-Sanchis, and Pekka Toivanen. Security threats in Zigbee-enabled systems: vulnerability evaluation, practical experiments, countermeasures, and lessons learned. In *System Sciences (HICSS), 2013 46th Hawaii International Conference on*, pages 5132–5138. IEEE, 2013.

144. Linus Wallgren, Shahid Raza, and Thiemo Voigt. Routing attacks and countermeasures in the rpl-based internet of things. *International Journal of Distributed Sensor Networks*, 9(8):794326, 2013.

145. Chen Wang, Xiaonan Guo, Yan Wang, Yingying Chen, and Bo Liu. Friend or foe?: Your wearable devices reveal your personal pin. In *Proceedings of the 11th ACM on Asia Conference on Computer and Communications Security*, pages 189–200. ACM, 2016.

146. He Wang, Ted Tsung-Te Lai, and Romit Roy Choudhury. Mole: Motion leaks through smartwatch sensors. In *Proceedings of the 21st Annual International Conference on Mobile Computing and Networking*, pages 155–166. ACM, 2015.

147. Rolf H Weber and Evelyne Studer. Cybersecurity in the internet of things: Legal aspects. *Computer Law & Security Review*, 32(5):715–728, 2016.

148. Biao Wei, Guohong Liao, Weijie Li, and Zheng Gong. A practical one-time file encryption protocol for iot devices. In *Computational Science and Engineering (CSE) and Embedded and Ubiquitous Computing (EUC), 2017 IEEE International Conference on*, volume 2, pages 114–119. IEEE, 2017.

149. Yi Wei, Karthik Sukumar, Christian Vecchiola, Dileban Karunamoorthy, and Rajkumar Buyya. Aneka cloud application platform and its integration with windows azure. *arXiv preprint arXiv:1103.2590*, 2011.

150. Jacob Wurm, Khoa Hoang, Orlando Arias, Ahmad-Reza Sadeghi, and Yier Jin. Security analysis on consumer and industrial iot devices. In *Design Automation Conference (ASP-DAC), 2016 21st Asia and South Pacific*, pages 519–524. IEEE, 2016.

151. Kun Yang, Domenic Forte, and Mark M Tehranipoor. Protecting endpoint devices in iot supply chain. In *Computer-Aided Design (ICCAD), 2015 IEEE/ACM International Conference on*, pages 351–356. IEEE, 2015.

152. Lijun Yang, Chao Ding, Meng Wu, and Kun Wang. Robust detection of false data injection attacks for the data aggregation in internet of things based environmental surveillance. *Computer Networks*, 2017.
153. Y. Yang, X. Liu, and R. H. Deng. Lightweight break-glass access control system for healthcare internet-of-things. *IEEE Transactions on Industrial Informatics*, pages 1–1, 2017.
154. Tianlong Yu, Vyas Sekar, Srinivasan Seshan, Yuvraj Agarwal, and Chenren Xu. Handling a trillion (unfixable) flaws on a billion devices: Rethinking network security for the internet-of-things. In *Proceedings of the 14th ACM Workshop on Hot Topics in Networks*, page 5. ACM, 2015.
155. Jonas Zaddach, Luca Bruno, Aurelien Francillon, and Davide Balzarotti. Avatar: A framework to support dynamic security analysis of embedded systems' firmwares. In *NDSS*, 2014.
156. Bruno Bogaz Zarpelão, Rodrigo Sanches Miani, Cláudio Toshio Kawakani, and Sean Carlisto de Alvarenga. A survey of intrusion detection in Internet of things. *Journal of Network and Computer Applications*, 2017.
157. Chi Zhang, Yanchao Zhang, and Yuguang Fang. Defending against physical destruction attacks on wireless sensor networks. In *Military Communications Conference, 2006. MIL-COM 2006. IEEE*, pages 1–7. IEEE, 2006.
158. Nan Zhang, Soteris Demetriou, Xianghang Mi, Wenrui Diao, Kan Yuan, Peiyuan Zong, Feng Qian, XiaoFeng Wang, Kai Chen, Yuan Tian, et al. Understanding iot security through the data crystal ball: Where we are now and where we are going to be. *arXiv preprint arXiv:1703.09809*, 2017.
159. Jun Zhao. On resilience and connectivity of secure wireless sensor networks under node capture attacks. *IEEE Transactions on Information Forensics and Security*, 12(3):557–571, 2017.
160. Charalambos Konstantinou and Michail Maniatakos Impact of firmware modification attacks on power systems field devices. *Smart Grid Communications (SmartGridComm), 2015 IEEE International Conference on*, 283–288, 2015.
161. YongBin Zhou and DengGuo Feng. Side-channel attacks: Ten years after its publication and the impacts on cryptographic module security testing. *IACR Cryptology ePrint Archive*, 2005:388, 2005.

Chapter 3
Towards Inferring IoT Maliciousness

The elaborated vulnerabilities undoubtedly open the door for adversaries to exploit IoT devices. While the provided taxonomy, discussed literature approaches and complementarity mitigation and awareness capabilities provide a unique, methodological approach to IoT security, in this chapter, we provide a concrete, first empirical perspective of Internet-wide IoT exploitations. To this end, we elaborate on the design, implementation and empirical evaluation of an approach for inferring Internet-scale IoT exploitations.

3.1 Inference of IoT Exploitation

In this section, we detail the approach which address the problem of inference of IoT exploitation and describe its aims, employed methods, and techniques. The proposed scheme is holistically illustrated in Fig. 3.1. In a nutshell, the approach endeavors to generate actionable cyber threat intelligence related to Internet-scale IoT devices by offering several data-driven methodologies, which mainly operate by scrutinizing passive empirical measurements. Such insights and inferences

This chapter was partially adopted from the works M. Galluscio, N. Neshenko, E. Bou-Harb, Y. Huang, N. Ghani, J. Crichigno, and G. Kaddoum. A first empirical look on internet-scale exploitations of iot devices. In *2017 IEEE 28th Annual International Symposium on Personal, Indoor, and Mobile Radio Communications (PIMRC)*, pages 1–7, Oct 2017.
Farooq Shaikh, Elias Bou-Harb, Nataliia Neshenko, Andrea P Wright, and Nasir Ghani. Internet of malicious things: correlating active and passive measurements for inferring and characterizing internet-scale unsolicited iot devices. *IEEE Communications Magazine*, 56(9):170–177, 2018.
Nataliia Neshenko, Martin Husák, Elias Bou-Harb, Pavel Čeleda, Sameera Al-Mulla, and Claude Fachkha. Data-driven intelligence for characterizing internet-scale iot exploitations. In *2018 IEEE Globecom Workshops (GC Wkshps)*, pages 1–7. IEEE, 2018.

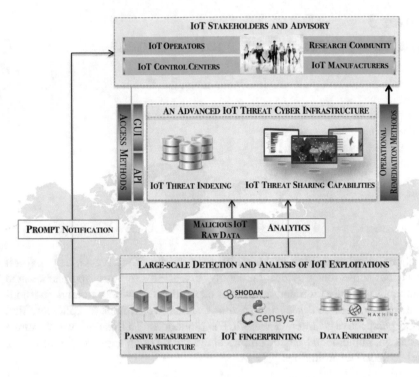

Fig. 3.1 Inferring and mitigating Internet-scale unsolicited IoT devices: a network telescope approach

are postulated to be distributed, in an operational cyber security fashion, to IoT stakeholders (i.e., operators, manufacturers, etc.) for prompt remediation and thus mitigation. Furthermore, an artifact of the envisioned approach is a repository, which aims at indexing malicious IoT empirical threat information (i.e., raw data and attack signatures) to be shared with the research and operational communities at large, hence facilitating advanced empirical IoT analytics as well as supporting further forensic investigations. In the sequel, we detail and elaborate on the components of the proposed approach.

3.1.1 Exploiting Darknet Data

Having access to empirical IoT data is indeed quite challenging. Several hurdles confirm the latter, including, the lack of visibility into local IoT realms due to logistic and privacy concerns, the general scarcity of malicious empirical data related to unsolicited IoT devices [9], and the lack of tangible IoT-specific attack signatures [17]. To this end, complementary methods ought to be explored; without access to tangible IoT empirical data, the notion of maliciousness in this context cannot be elaborated. In this work, we uniquely exploit passive measurements rendered by analyzing darknet data to achieve the latter task. A darknet (also commonly referred to as a network telescope) is a set of routable and allocated yet unused IP addresses [5, 16]. It represents a partial view of the entire Internet address space. From a design perspective, a darknet is transparent and indistinguishable compared with the rest of the Internet space. From a deployment perspective, it is rendered by network sensors that are implemented and dispersed on numerous strategic points throughout the Internet. Such sensors are often distributed and are typically hosted by various global entities, including Internet Service Providers (ISPs), academic and research facilities, and backbone networks. The aim of a darknet is to provide a lens on Internet-wide unsolicited traffic; since darknet IP addresses are unused, any traffic targeting them represents anomalous traffic [2]. Figure 3.2 illustrates a common darknet architecture. In this work, we exploit network telescopes to identify network traffic originating from unsolicited IoT devices. The rationale here, as illustrated in Fig. 3.2, is rendered by our initial empirical observations, which concur that compared with typical Internet hosts/machines, exploited IoT devices will also attempt to either propagate to infect other Internet IoT devices by launching scanning activities towards the Internet space, or fall victims of Distributed DoS (DDoS) attacks. In either case, depending on the vantage points of the employed network telescopes, a varied portion of such activities will indeed target such dark IP spaces. To this end, well-established algorithms, methods, and techniques could be leveraged, which scrutinize darknet data (also known as Internet

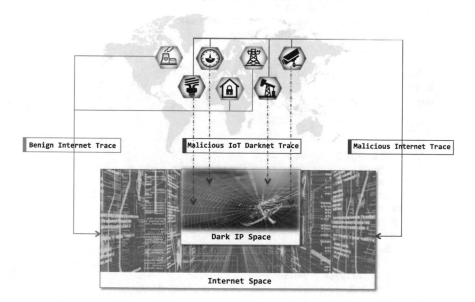

Fig. 3.2 Network telescopes capturing Internet-scale IoT unsolicited traffic

Background Radiation (IBR)) to fingerprint such activities and thus infer sources of unsolicited IoT devices in addition to extracting their corresponding darknet traffic traces. For instance, such algorithms could be based on threshold analysis to infer IoT-generated scanning activities or exploit backscattered packet analysis (i.e., the analysis of reply packets originating from victims of DDoS attacks that were targeted by spoofed attackers) to pinpoint IoT devices that have been targeted by DDoS attacks [6].

3.1.2 Probing Inference

To infer probing activities from darknet data, we present Algorithm 1, which exploits flow-based parameters. Algorithm 1 operates on darknet flows, which are defined by a series of consecutive packets sharing the same source IP address. The algorithm counts the number of packets per flow to measure the rate of the suspicious activities within a certain time window (Tw). If the flow packet count (pkt_cnt) is beyond a specific threshold, the flow is deemed as a probe. To this end, we employ the packet count threshold from [12], defined by 64 probed darknet addresses on the same port. Please note, that typically, the probing engine would have also required and established a rate threshold (Rth). Nevertheless, we do

---

Algorithm 1 Probing inference algorithm

1: **Input:** A set (F) of unique darknet flows (f),
2: Each flow f contains packet count (pkt_cnt) and rate ($rate$)
   Tw: Time window
   Pth: Packet threshold
   Rth: Rate threshold,
   Tn: Time of packet number n in a flow
   pkt: Packet
   Output: Probing flag, Pr_flag
3:
4: **for** Each f in F **do**
5:    $pkt\_cnt \leftarrow 0$
6:    $T1 \leftarrow$ pkt_gettime()
7:    $Tf \leftarrow T1 + Tw$
8:    **while** pkt in f **do**
9:       $Tn=$ pkt_gettime()
10:      **if** $Tn < Tf$ **then**
11:         pkt_cnt $\leftarrow$ pkt_cnt + 1
12:      **end if**
13:   **end while**
14:   $rate \leftarrow \frac{pkt\_cnt}{Tw}$
15:   **if** $pkt\_cnt > Pth$ & $rate > Rth$ **then**
16:      $Pr\_flag() \leftarrow 1$
17:   **end if**
18: **end for**
----

not enforce one here, to enable the algorithm to infer very low rate, possible stealthy activities. Indeed, the approach embedded in Algorithm 1 would fingerprint Internet-scale probing traces. Please note that from a performance perspective, when implemented "on the fly" on the darknet data stream using the C libpcap library [8], the developed inference algorithm can process close to 10,000 flows in approximately 1 min (average throughput of 150 flows/s).

3.1.3   Correlation with Active Measurements

To infer probes that have been specifically generated from exploited IoT devices, one needs to fingerprint IoT generated traffic. Indeed, such task is currently an open research problem and very few endeavors (if not nil) have addressed it. While the efficiency of fingerprinting techniques that identify IoT devices by observing Internet traffic are continuously evolving [7, 15], their advance is not yet sufficient to address identification task in the large-scale. In this work, we approach this issue from a different perspective by leveraging active measurements. This entitles executing Internet-wide scanning, capturing the results and filtering the replies from the destinations based on their nature. Fortunately, the Shodan service [13] performs the latter and indexes online IoT devices. To this end, we leverage Shodan's available database of IoT devices, which are deployed in both, consumer environments as well as in CPS realms. We retrieve online IoT devices and correlate them using their source IP information with IP data retrieved by conducting probing analysis of the darknet data as previously mentioned. More specifically, given a list of source IP addresses extracted from darknet traffic, and a list of IoT-specific IP addresses extracted from the IoT databases, the correlation algorithm performs linear search to infer a match. Please note that the current proposed approach operates in an offline mode. Future work will explore auxiliary online approaches to permit the near real-time inference of Internet-scale compromised devices. Thus, one core outcome of such proposed approach are inferred Internet-scale exploited IoT devices, which are attempting to scan other Internet hosts (to fingerprint or exploit them). Indeed, such correlation faces several challenges. First, in terms of darknet data, there is a need to sanitize such data to filter out misconfiguration traffic. Such traffic is the result of software, hardware or routing errors which direct erroneous packets to the darknet. Second, in terms of the Shodan IoT database, one obstacle is the strenuous process to identify relevant IoT information (i.e., types, IP addresses, etc.) and properly curate (download, sanitize and store) the obtained information. Third, in terms of the actual correlation procedure, the design of the algorithm that executes the correlation should be optimized to perform efficient searches.

Auxiliary outcomes, which are currently work in progress, include (1) accessing IoT malicious empirical data which can be extracted from darknet data and shared at large with the research community to facilitate forensic investigations of IoT-relevant data, and (2) generating tangible IoT-specific attack signatures, using tools such as `ssdeep` [11], which can be deployed at local IoT realms to aid with the task of prompt mitigation.

3.1.4   Generating IoT-Specific Malicious Signatures

Currently, there exists a substantial lack of tangible malicious empirical indicators in the context of IoT [17]. This is mainly due to physical and logistic constraints that are strictly enforced by IoT operators in various realms. Additionally, data gathering and analytics efforts, which aim at addressing the distributed and the heterogeneous nature of the IoT paradigm, are still in their infancy. Along these lines, it becomes highly imperative to generate such notions, which could aid in various IoT cyber security research and development endeavors. Indeed, the proposed approach was specifically designed in a manner to facilitate the generation of such artifacts. In particular, by executing network traffic correlations between passive and the results of active Internet measurements, we obtain access to rare unsolicited network traffic traces originating from Internet-scale compromised IoT devices. To this end, one imperative output would be to generate malicious IoT signatures, which characterize such extracted traces. These signatures are envisioned to be (1) employed on newly-incoming darknet sessions to fingerprint unsolicited IoT devices that have not been previously indexed by databases such as Shodan and Censys, and (2) distributed to local IoT realms where they can be deployed in traditional Intrusion Detection Systems (IDSs) to support future, proactive IoT inference and mitigation. To mutually support the aforementioned two objectives, in this work, we exploit the concept of fuzzy hashing through tailoring and applying the Context Triggered Piecewise Hashing (CTPH) algorithm [4] on darknet traces that have been generated by the inferred unsolicited IoT devices. In particular, the IP header information is utilized in this context. The CTPH technique is advantageous in comparison with typical hashing, as it can provide a percentage of similarity rather than solely providing a binary output. This is particularly beneficial in the context of the first objective; where we apply the generated signatures on darknet traffic traces to verify if they possess some degree of similarity in comparison with previously obtained traces per the proposed approach of Sect. 3.1.3.

The CTPH algorithm operates only in the current context of the input, maintaining its state based solely on the last few bytes of the data file, thus producing a pseudo-random value as output. Essentially, the algorithm generates discrete hashes by dividing the file into multiple segments and computing hashes for these segments instead of computing a single hash for the entire file. In this way, localized segment changes do not affect the hashes for the rest of the file, and a degree of similarity can be determined in the case of almost identical files. The CTPH algorithm employs a rolling hash technique based upon Alder32 checksum [4], which is computed for each data byte in the concerned file. This process is continuously iterated until all the bytes of the input file have been processed to generate the final signature. Readers that are interested in more details related to the CTPH algorithm are kindly referred to [4].

3.2 Empirical Evaluation

In this section, we employ the proposed approach of Sect. 3.1 to elaborate on the generated insights and inferences. We begin with our first attempt ever to comprehend the severity of IoT maliciousness by empirically characterizing the magnitude of Internet-scale IoT exploitations. We further continue with an analysis of generated by unsolicited IoT devices traffic to create effective mitigation signatures that could be deployed at local IoT realms. Finally, we generate amalgamated statistics regarding compromised devices and their hosting environments, including sector information, which has never been reported before.

3.2.1 First Empirical Look on Internet-Scale Exploitation of IoT Devices

We exploit close to 130 GB of darknet data that was recently retrieved in the month of June 2017. We executed queries using the Shodan service to index online IoT devices, which are deployed in both, consumer and CPS environments. On one hand, for the IoT consumer market, we focused on five categories, namely, IoT cameras, Digital Video Recorders (DVRs), routers, printers and home media servers. We chose the latter as they seemed to be widely deployed and well adopted in addition to showing a history of exploitation (as in the case of the Mirai malware abusing IP cameras and DVRs). In total, we have indexed 862,014 IoT consumer devices that were online at the time of writing of this chapter. On the other hand, from the CPS perspective, we focused on six sectors as summarized in Table 3.1.

In total, we were able to index 72,554 IoT devices which have been deployed and operated in those CPS sectors. Figure 3.3a, b illustrate the distribution of such IoT

Table 3.1 IoT devices related to various CPS deployments

CPS sector	Protocol
Building automation	BACnet, Tridium
Factory automation	CoDeSys
Industrial automation	Red Lion Controls, Siemens-S7, MELSEC-Q
Manufacturing	OMRON, EtherNet/IP
Power utilities	Modbus
Water facilities	DNP3

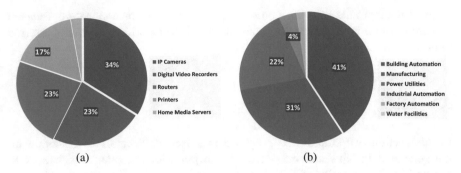

Fig. 3.3 Distribution of IoT devices deployed in consumer and CPS realms. (**a**) Consumer sectors. (**b**) CPS sectors

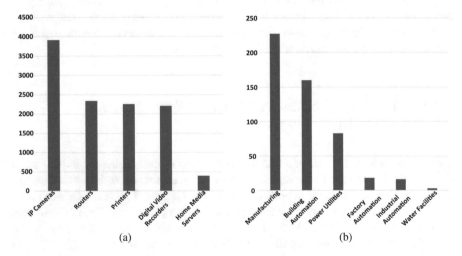

Fig. 3.4 Distribution of **exploited** IoT devices deployed in consumer and CPS realms. (**a**) Consumer sectors. (**b**) CPS sectors

devices in their numerous corresponding realms. It can be extracted that IoT devices related to IP cameras, DVRs and routers are quite well deployed. Further, it can be inferred that IoT devices in building automation facilities, manufacturing plants and power utilities render the majority of the IoT deployments.

We proceed by invoking the inference algorithm and the correlation procedure as briefed in Sects. 3.1.2 and 3.1.3. The outcome uncovers Internet-scale compromised IoT devices in various sectors. Overall, we were able to infer 11,122 exploited IoT devices related to the consumer sector, while the results further disclosed 510 vulnerable IoT devices in critical CPS sectors. Figure 3.4a, b illustrate the distribution of such exploitations within their corresponding categories. While the exploitation of IoT cameras is a reasonable outcome, DVRs, which have been exploited earlier this year by the Mirai malware, do not seem to be on top of the list of most exploited. In fact, IoT routers and printers appear to be more heavily compromised. This questions the fact if such devices will soon be leveraged as new bots within numerous botnets to launch similarly devastating attacks towards high priority Internet assets. More alarming, the results also demonstrate that IoT devices in manufacturing plants, building automation facilities and power utilities are the most exploited. This is indeed quite worrying, given that such vulnerabilities not only could lead to theft of highly sensitive and possibly classified intellectual property, but can also cause issues to the power infrastructure of nations and even endanger human life. By performing geo-location procedures using maxmind [14], we were able to attribute such IoT exploitations deployed in various CPS realms to their hosting environments (i.e., ISPs and countries). Please note that since we are exploiting probing intelligence as indicators of exploitation, the sources render real, non-spoofed IP addresses [3]. Figure 3.5 reveals that China, the United States, Canada and Spain host the top most IoT exploitations while Fig. 3.6 shows the top six corresponding ISPs hosting these compromised IoT devices.

To the best of our knowledge, the generated results herein render a first attempt ever to shed the light on Internet-scale IoT maliciousness. Indeed, empowered with such cyber threat intelligence, one can share such information with local IoT realms which are hosting these compromised IoT devices for prompt eradication, thus providing effective IoT mitigation. It is noteworthy to mention that the overall ratio

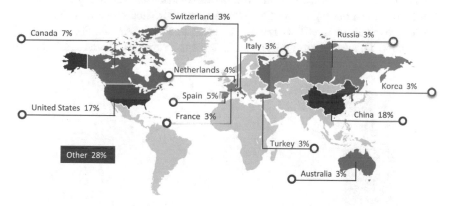

Fig. 3.5 Internet-scale distribution of **exploited** IoT devices deployed in CPS realms

Fig. 3.6 Top 6 ISPs hosting **compromised** IoT devices in CPS realms

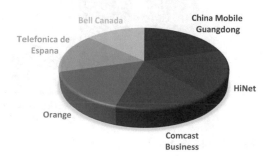

between sampled (i.e., deployed) IoT devices and inferred exploited IoT devices in both, the consumer market and CPS realms, is computed to be around 2%. While this number seem to be small, one should note that IoT projections for 2020 is expected to reach 50 billion online IoT device, thus ominously causing IoT exploitations to develop into a momentous cyber security distress, to say the least.

3.2.2 Characterization and Signature Generation

We exploit passive Internet-scale darknet data in conjunction with active measurements provided by Shodan and Censys to infer the presence of malicious IoT devices, which have been deployed in consumer realms as well as in critical systems. In total, we analyzed close to 1.5 TB of darknet data to verify the infection status of 275,478 IoT devices. The darknet data analyzed was for the months of November and December 2016 as well as January and February 2017 whereas the IoT IP addresses were retrieved from Shodan and Censys for the month of December 2016. For the sake of this work, we have investigated five categories of IoT devices, including, Digital Video Recorders (DVRs), webcams, thermostats, Bluetooth-enabled devices in addition to IoT sensors deployed deep in control automation systems. Figure 3.7 illustrates the distribution of analyzed devices within their corresponding categories. Overall, we extracted close to 165,000 IoT device deployed in various Supervisory Control and Data Acquisition (SCADA) environments. This category represented 55% of the extracted devices. DVRs and

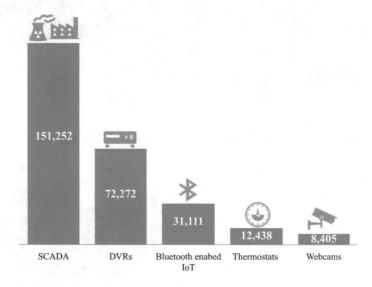

Fig. 3.7 Distribution of investigated IoT devices by type

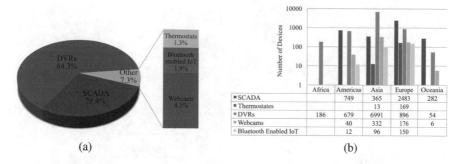

Fig. 3.8 Distribution of exploited IoT devices. (a) By types. (b) By type and region

Bluetooth-enabled IoT devices were less present, covering close to 26% and 11% of the total number of devices, respectively. The remaining 8% of investigated devices rendered IoT webcams and thermostats.

We proceeded by executing the correlation algorithm between passive and active measurements, as described in Sect. 3.1. The results unveiled the presence of almost 14,000 Internet-scale, currently active compromised IoT devices. We also note that close to 20% of such IoT devices were indeed found to be victims of DDoS attacks compared to those that have been inferred as generating scanning activities. Indeed, such outcome validates our intuition that there exists a significant number of IoT devices that are involved in malicious activities in addition to corroborating our hypothesis that exploring network telescope traffic is an effective methodology to shed the light on Internet-scale IoT maliciousness.

We proceeded by characterizing such exploited IoT devices as illustrated in Fig. 3.8a. We observed that DVRs occupied a significant portion (64.3%) of compromised IoT devices; a result which corroborates the exploitation of such devices earlier this year by the Mirai malware to launch debilitating DDoS attacks on Dyn DNS servers, which paralyzed part of the Internet infrastructure. IoT devices deployed in SCADA realms (mostly belonging to building automation systems, power utilities, and manufacturing plants) occupied 28.4% of the total share of unsolicited devices found in the darknet. IoT webcams, thermostats and other Bluetooth-enabled devices were also shown to be compromised. Indeed, such inferences could promptly be leveraged by the operational cyber security community (i.e., IoT operators and manufacturers, cyber situational response teams, etc.) to aid in the rapid notification and thus mitigation of such exploitations.

To characterize the hosting environments of such IoT exploitations, we executed geo-location procedures by employing the maxmind GeoIP2 database [14]. Our analysis revealed that the majority of compromised IoT devices are located in Asia followed by Europe and the Americas as depicted in Fig. 3.8b.

Asia was found to host a significant number of malicious DVRs, while exploited IoT devices deployed in control automation realms were mostly deployed in Europe and the Americas. Webcams and thermostats had a significantly smaller share when compared to DVRs and SCADA IoT devices and were distributed between Asia

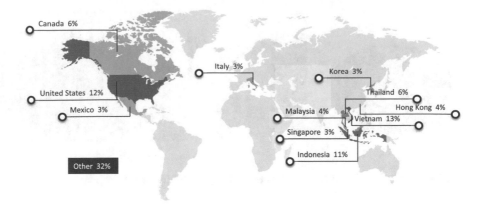

Fig. 3.9 Global distribution of exploited IoT devices

Table 3.2 Signatures for fingerprinting unsolicited IoT devices

Device	Signature
DVR	12288:wsIGM8PFc6fXPWW4cVsBK0GT5gkLXI5aurnz9k/Kk6: wsIP8i6fPWW4cmBKrT5gkzIxrnz9+Kk6
Webcam	3072:6OA062aJtmzOTYfpTYJ7JaZgVx3BAaTZQzTwcht79+ 8R+TMWs9Zm2g0ivLJ1p/jR:rgFmQyTEJaQmzTwM1982g0YF111YaJ
Printer	24576:XH9m8fEgLoZ7EqC0kf7tzH2uF/SD6dcZwEmGOqzH9m8fEgLf:4
Thermostat	6144:cMKa4Umz8VNPTg80mL4STGDs3+5FIwnVTF3gjGzTkpB/ JkmB1DRkXY574OM231PL:0V80fJow3gIAJkmQ 23I8eme/X4AMG6Bb

and Europe. Figure 3.9 depicts the worldwide distribution of top countries hosting exploited IoT devices. Intuitively, this outcome is affected by the selected and investigated IoT IP addresses, the specific darknet data sample that has been utilized, and the time frame of the executed analysis. We also generate further, more precise geo-location information such as hosting organization and ISPs, though we do not expose such results for sensitivity reasons.

We also generate IoT-specific malicious signatures per the proposed approach of Sect. 3.1.4 by executing the CTPH algorithm on extracted IP header information from darknet traffic related to compromised IoT devices. To successfully achieve this, we leverage an open source implementation of the algorithm, namely, the ssdeep utility [10]. A sample of such signatures, related to four different IoT devices, for proof-of-concept purposes, is summarized in Table 3.2.

Such signatures render a first attempt ever to capture notions of IoT malicious by scrutinizing empirical data. Please recall that these signatures are postulated to be deployed on newly-incoming darknet traces to fingerprint newly exploited IoT devices that have not been previously indexed by certain databases such as Shodan and Censys. Moreover, these signatures could be employed at local IoT realms to aid in the mitigation and thus remediation objectives.

3.2.3   A Closer Look into Hosting Environment

In this section, we provide a characterization of IoT maliciousness in terms of illicit activities and hosting environments. The executed analysis draws upon close to 1.2 TB of darknet data that was collected from a /8 network telescope provided by CAIDA [1] for a recent 24-h period. We distinguish two classes of maliciousness presented in this period. These are (1) victims of DDoS attacks, including victims of TCP, UDP, and ICMP flooding; and (2) hosts that conduct horizontal, vertical, and strobe scans against Internet hosts. Precisely, we identified close to 5000 Internet hosts that have fallen victims of more than 30,000 DDoS attacks. We also identified nearly 1.2 million infected hosts, which generated 4.5 million scanning activities.

The correlation algorithm between network telescope traffic and the IoT dataset yielded nearly 56,000 IoT devices, which generated illicit Internet traffic, representing 5% of total inferred malicious activities. Auxiliary, nearly 940 IoT devices fell victims of 9000 DDoS attacks. It is worthy to pinpoint that IoT devices presented 19% of the total identified DDoS victims. In the same manner, 5% of the infected Internet hosts that attempted to explore other Internet hosts are IoT devices, which generated 9% of total scans. The latter is an alarming number of IoT malicious activities taking into account that we only analyzed 1 day of network telescope traffic. We identified the presence of compromised IoT devices in 169 countries worldwide, hosted by 39 various business sectors, in nearly 4000 ISPs. Figure 3.10 illustrates the global distribution of such unsolicited IoT devices and emphasizes the top 5 source countries. Specifically, we detected devices in China (49%), followed by Brazil (8%), United States (3%), South Korea (3%), and Russia (3%). In total, these countries hosted 66% of the affected devices, which generated close to 51% of the inferred illicit activities.

The significant number of IoT-generated malicious activities was found to be associated with various hosting sectors, such as Internet service providers (40%)

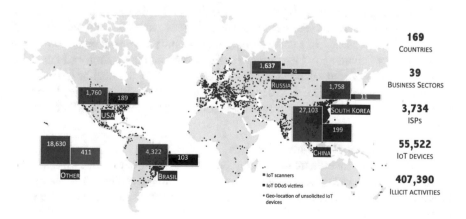

Fig. 3.10 IoT devices: global exploitations and DoS victims

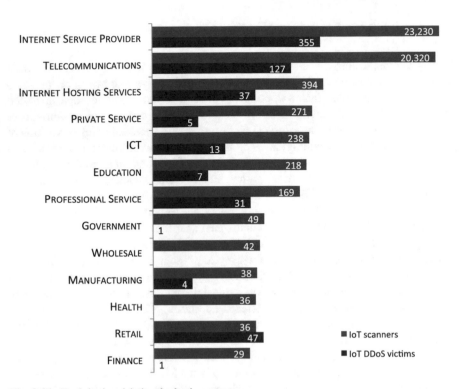

Fig. 3.11 Exploitations/victims by business sectors

and telecommunication entities (30%), which hosted 42% and 36% of compromised devices, respectively. Figure 3.11 illustrates the most affected hosting sectors and their corresponding number of misdemeanors.

While the aim of the aforementioned IoT-specific malicious activities is unclear, the presence of such devices in educational, governmental and professional services could be benign (for research purposes). Additionally, despite the relatively low number of compromised devices in critical sectors such as manufacturing and financial, their presence in such sectors is significantly alarming and could cause serious issues, including exfiltration of sensitive data and environmental damages. Auxiliary, we observed unsolicited IoT devices hosted in the healthcare industry. The stolen information from such devices could cause momentous privacy breaches, fraudulent insurance claims, and more severely, such exploitations could threaten patients' lives.

IoT Devices Conducting Network Scans
In this section, we investigate the hosting environments of IoT devices which were found to be aggressively scanning the Internet space. We center our investigation around the five countries that hosted the highest number of IoT devices. The latter devices generated 50% of total scanning activities from around 66% of the total volume of affected IoT nodes. Table 3.3 summarizes the activities of such devices by country.

Table 3.3 Number of infected IoT devices and scanning activities by country

Country	Devices	Scans	Scans/Device
China	27,103	98,444	3.63
Brazil	4,322	38,516	8.91
United States	1,760	21,106	11.99
South Korea	1,758	29,436	16.74
Russia	1,637	13,891	8.49
Other countries	18,630	197,347	10.59

Table 3.4 Top ISPs hosting the most IoT exploitations

ISP	Devices	Scans	Scans/Device
Vivo	3105	23,662	7.62
China Mobile Guangdong	2978	7805	2.62
China Unicom Liaoning	2818	10,757	3.82
China Telecom Guangdong	2017	6091	3.02
China Telecom Jiangsu	1569	5628	3.59
China Telecom	1556	7332	4.71
China Telecom Zhejiang	1343	4496	3.35
China Telecom Sichuan	1238	3169	2.56
China Telecom Fujian	1237	6922	5.6
China Telecom Hunan	905	3870	4.28
Other ISPs	17,814	121,661	6.83

   The average rate of scanning activities per one compromised device indicates that devices which are located in South Korea and the US generate malicious traffic more aggressively than those which were found in China, the country with the highest number of compromised devices. Deliberate examination of this rate uncovered that the most aggressive scan activities are generated by few devices hosted by numerous business sectors, including, ISPs, the US government, health, education, and the financial sector (in particular banks). In South Korea, the majority of such illicit events are hosted by telecommunication companies and IPSs. The study of ISPs in the countries with the highest presence of unsolicited IoT devices uncovered that Vivo, the larger telecommunications company in Brazil, appears to be number one host of unsolicited IoT devices, presented by 6% of total compromised devices. Further, 5% of compromised devices are hosted by China Mobile Guangdong, China Unicom Liaoning and China Telecom Guangdong. Table 3.4 lists the top 10 ISPs which host the most IoT compromised devices.

Table 3.5 Number of IoT DDoS victims and attacks by country

Country	Devices	Attacks	Attack/Device
China	199	3,033	15.24
United States	189	1,579	8.35
Brazil	103	674	6.54
Russia	24	131	5.46
South Korea	11	54	4.91
Other countries	411	3,179	7.73

Table 3.6 Top 4 ISPs hosting IoT DDoS victims in China

ISP	Devices	Attacks	Attack/Device
China Telecom backbone network	75	1631	21.75
China Telecom Shanghai	18	332	18.44
China Telecom	16	308	19.25
China Telecom Shandong	10	162	16.2
Other ISPs	80	600	7.5

IoT Devices as DDoS Victims

In this section, we investigate the hosting environments of IoT devices which have fallen victims of DDoS attacks. Such devices were identified as representing 63% of total number of inferred DDoS attacks in the aforementioned top countries. In fact, these attacks affected 56% of inferred devices. Table 3.5 specifies the number of IoT DDoS victims and attacks by country.

Please note that attack/device represents the average number of attacks per IoT device, and not the magnitude of such attacks. In this context, we observed that the devices in China attracted the highest number of illicit activities. Precisely, their number is twice higher than in other countries. A closer investigation of this fact unveiled that the significant number of such devices is associated with 4 ISPs that have suffered persistent attacks. In fact, these ISPs, which are listed in Table 3.6, hosted 60% of IoT DDoS victims in China, absorbing close to 80% of attacks, as observed by the monitored network telescope.

The study of ISPs in the aforementioned countries uncovered that the ISP which hosted a significant number of DDoS victims is SNH Servicos de Internet Ltda., which is an Internet provider in Brazil. The closest follower is China Telecom backbone network. Table 3.7 summarizes the top 5 ISPs that were found to be hosting the highest number of IoT DDoS victims.

Table 3.7 ISPs hosting IoT DDoS victims in countries with the highest number of IoT exploitations

ISP	Devices	Attacks
SNH Servicos de Internet Ltda.	90	463
China Telecom backbone network	75	1631
AT&T U-verse	40	641
Google	34	134
Amazon Technologies	25	119
Other ISPs	238	2352

References

1. UCSD Network Telescope – Near-Real-Time Network Telescope Dataset. [Online]. Available: http://www.caida.org/data/passive/telescope-near-real-time_dataset.xml. Accessed 2018-03-05.
2. Elias Bou-Harb, Nour-Eddine Lakhdari, Hamad Binsalleeh, and Mourad Debbabi. Multidimensional investigation of source port 0 probing. *Digital Investigation*, 11:S114–S123, 2014.
3. Bou-Harb, Elias and Debbabi, Mourad and Assi, Chadi. Cyber scanning: a comprehensive survey. *IEEE Communications Surveys & Tutorials*, 16(3):1496–1519, 2014.
4. Lianhua Chi and Xingquan Zhu. Hashing techniques: A survey and taxonomy. *ACM Computing Surveys (CSUR)*, 50(1):11, 2017.
5. Claude Fachkha and Mourad Debbabi. Darknet as a source of cyber intelligence: Survey, taxonomy, and characterization. *IEEE Communications Surveys and Tutorials*, 18(2):1197–1227, 2016.
6. Claude Fachkha and Mourad Debbabi. Darknet as a source of cyber intelligence: Survey, taxonomy, and characterization. *IEEE Communications Surveys & Tutorials*, 18(2):1197–1227, 2016.
7. David Formby, Preethi Srinivasan, Andrew Leonard, Jonathan Rogers, and Raheem Beyah. Who's in control of your control system? device fingerprinting for cyber-physical systems. In *Network and Distributed System Security Symposium (NDSS)*, 2016.
8. Luis Martin Garcia. Programming with libpcap-sniffing the network from our own application. *Hakin9-Computer Security Magazine*, pages 2–2008, 2008.
9. Dina Hadžiosmanović, Robin Sommer, Emmanuele Zambon, and Pieter H Hartel. Through the eye of the PLC: semantic security monitoring for industrial processes. In *Proceedings of the 30th Annual Computer Security Applications Conference*, pages 126–135. ACM, 2014.
10. Jesse Kornblum. ssdeep - Fuzzy hashing program. [Online]. Available: http://ssdeep.sourceforge.net/. Accessed 2018-03-05.
11. Jesse Kornblum. Identifying almost identical files using context triggered piecewise hashing. *Digital investigation*, 3:91–97, 2006.
12. Lukas Krämer, Johannes Krupp, Daisuke Makita, Tomomi Nishizoe, Takashi Koide, Katsunari Yoshioka, and Christian Rossow. Amppot: Monitoring and defending against amplification ddos attacks. In *Research in Attacks, Intrusions, and Defenses*, pages 615–636. Springer, 2015.
13. J Matherly. Shodan search engine. [Online]. Available: https://www.shodan.io. Accessed 2018-03-05.
14. MaxMind, Inc. GeoIP2 Databases. [Online]. Available: https://www.maxmind.com/en/geoip2-databases. Accessed 2018-03-05.

15. Yair Meidan, Michael Bohadana, Asaf Shabtai, Juan David Guarnizo, Martín Ochoa, Nils Ole Tippenhauer, and Yuval Elovici.   Profiliot: a machine learning approach for iot device identification based on network traffic analysis. In *Proceedings of the Symposium on Applied Computing*, pages 506–509. ACM, 2017.
16. David Moore, Colleen Shannon, Geoffrey M Voelker, and Stefan Savage. *Network telescopes: Technical report*. Department of Computer Science and Engineering, University of California, San Diego, 2004.
17. Tianlong Yu, Vyas Sekar, Srinivasan Seshan, Yuvraj Agarwal, and Chenren Xu. Handling a trillion (unfixable) flaws on a billion devices: Rethinking network security for the internet-of-things. In *Proceedings of the 14th ACM Workshop on Hot Topics in Networks*, page 5. ACM, 2015.

Chapter 4
Generating and Sharing IoT-Centric Cyber Threat Intelligence

To achieve our goals of generating intelligence for large-scale IoT exploitations, we designed and implemented an automated platform, namely Siot. The aim of the platform is to automate the collection and analysis of relevant data to infer unsolicited IoT devices and its hosting environments, in near real-time. Figure 4.1 illustrates the framework of the Siot platform. Explicitly, the modules are designed to achieve the following tasks:

- aggregation and analysis of malicious activities detected in the network telescope to infer unsolicited activities of IoT devices;
- identification of corresponding hosting environments;
- estimation of indicators of a highly exploited hosting countries, business sectors, and ISPs to provide early warnings regarding such exploitations;
- generation of various dynamic dashboards (i.e., front-end) which facilitate analysis of IoT hostility.

To this end, the aggregation component takes as input scanning and DDoS flows, revealed by employing backscatter and probing algorithms (Sects. 3.1.1 and 3.1.2) on darknet data, which was collected from a /8 network telescope by CAIDA [2]. The input then is extensively analysed (Sects. 3.1.3 and 3.1.4) to produce intelligence related to large-scale IoT exploitations. The latter empowers operation and research community with the capability to detect and mitigate compromised IoT devices, and provide insights for preventing further exploitations.

In the sequel, we detail and elaborate on the components of the platform which is a web server (server-side) and web application client (client-side), as illustrated in Fig. 4.2.

4.1 Server Core Function

The main functions of the Siot platform consist of data aggregation and data processing modules along with various auxiliary support functions.

© Springer Nature Switzerland AG 2020
E. Bou-Harb, N. Neshenko, *Cyber Threat Intelligence for the Internet of Things*,
https://doi.org/10.1007/978-3-030-45858-4_4

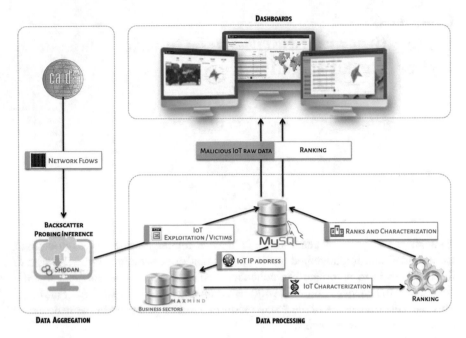

Fig. 4.1 Framework of the Siot platform for inferring and characterizing Internet-scale exploitations

4.1.1   Data Aggregation Module

The core function of the data aggregation module is to infer IoT exploitations and DDoS victims. To this end, it extracts IP addresses from the DDoS and scan flows and correlate them with IoT search engine Shodan by employing its API [4]. Please note that currently probing inference and backscatter algorithms operate in a separate module. Future work will explore integration approaches to permit the near real-time inference of Internet-scale compromised devices.

4.1.2   Data Processing Module

This module is responsible for the identification of the hosting environments of unsolicited IoT devices, and providing warning indicators for highly exploited areas. The latter warrant proper mitigation at large-scale. To this end, this module correlates each IP address associated with the unsolicited IoT devices with internal and external databases. In this context, we utilized internal knowledge (gathered by conducting discussions with numerous Internet entities) rendered by IP ranges associated with various business sectors. Complementary, we employed maxmind [3]

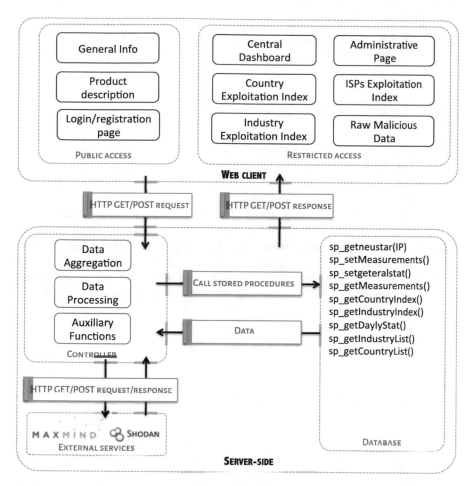

Fig. 4.2 Components of the `Siot` platform for inferring and characterizing Internet-scale exploitations

for the remaining geolocation requirements. Further, the ranking functions calculate three compound indices, namely

1. Country exploitation index
2. Industry exploitation index
3. ISP exploitation index

Indeed, such indices significantly simplify monitoring and comparison the severity level of IoT exploitation in various contexts. Each index includes two indicators, such as (1) rank by the number of exploited devices, (2) rank by the number of unsolicited activities conducted by the compromised devices. The rank is presented as a score from 1 to 10, where 1 refers to the lowest severity level of IoT exploitation, while 10 represents its highest degree.

It is worthy to pinpoint that we selected the index based on the criteria of data availability and its quality. In this context, we leave the index of IoT type exploitation for future work.

4.1.3   Auxiliary Functions

The auxiliary functions are responsible for (1) database access, insuring that all requests are processed reliably and securely, whereas multiple simultaneous inquiries are appropriately queued; (2) identity and access management, ensuring secure data access and isolation of various processes.

An identity and access management component grants the users access to the platform modules consistent with the users' roles. It takes as input the login credentials provided by a user through the login form and sends the request to the server to check whether the requested access is legitimate. If the combination of the login and password contained in the request message exists, the server returns the user information and the assigned web page according to the user's role. In this context, the user without administrative privilege cannot access the corresponding page and is rerouted directly to the central dashboard. A logout component clears the user session and forwards the users' to a publicly accessible page.

4.2   Client-Side Core Components

Users interact with the `Siot` platform through various front-end interfaces which are login/logout, administrator control panel, and several interactive dashboards. These include a central dashboard, country exploitation index panel, industry exploitation index dashboard, hosting ISPs analytics, and access to raw data. The input and output of the user components above are HTTP POST request and response messages.

We describe each user interface above in greater detail in this section.

Login/Logout
All users have access to public pages such as the platform index page and product information. To gain restricted access to the dashboards of IoT malicious activities or administrator control panel, the users provide credentials through the login page.

Administrator Control Panel
An administrator control panel allows a user to activate data processing functions as well as display general statistics regarding available data.

Dashboards
This component generates various dynamic dashboards which facilitate analysis of IoT hostility. All dashboards are implemented using JavaServer Pages (JSP)

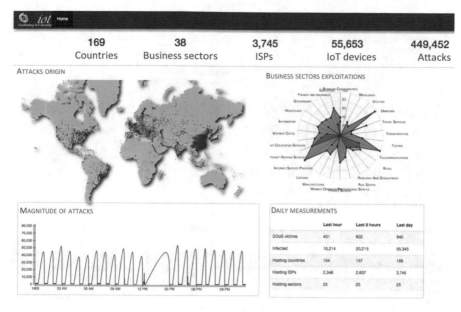

Fig. 4.3 A screenshot of the central dashboard

and the JavaScript library, known as Data Driven Documents or D3 [1]. The user interfaces, in turn, are implemented using HTML, SVG, and CSS. By producing the dashboards, we make available all indexed IoT malicious raw data and the generated inferences. To this end, the dynamic nature of the dashboards allows filtering indexed data and drilling down to the lowest data level which is related to the IP addresses of compromised devices. The latter permits the users to investigate IoT hostility from general to specific characteristics. Figure 4.3 illustrates the central dashboard which provides the users amalgamated statistics regarding compromised IoT devices and their hosting environments.

The central dashboard provides the users quick links to the panels with indicators of exploitation in various contexts, including hosting countries, business sectors, and ISPs. In this context, Fig. 4.4 displays a screenshot of the dashboard with country exploitation index. The streamlined nature of the dashboard allows filtering the country index by selecting different types of attacks against IoT, searching a specific country in a table, and retrieving details regarding IoT exploitation in the country chosen by clicking the respective record in the table, as illustrated in Fig. 4.5. Besides, users could access industry exploitation index for a selected country. In a similar fashion, users could get access to amalgamated statistics regarding the exploitation index of business sectors, as illustrated in Fig. 4.6. Moreover, users can analyze this index in the context of different countries. Similar insights are generated in the context of ISPs. Last but not least, users can filter information by device IP, hosting country, business sector, and ISP from a panel with raw malicious data. All filters employ "and/or" operations.

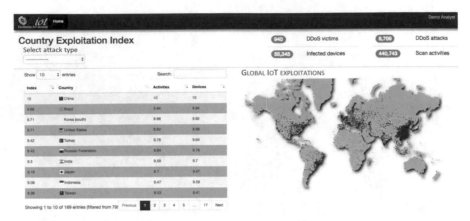

Fig. 4.4   A screenshot of country exploitation index dashboard

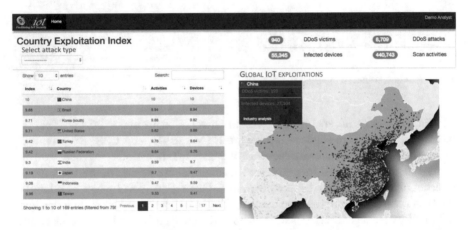

Fig. 4.5   A detailing dashboard perspective on the country exploitation index

4.3   Performance Evaluation

In this section, we evaluate the performance of the implemented platform. Our prime interest in this evaluation is the throughput of the platform.

Although we designed our platform to be deployed as "security-as-as-service" in the cloud, the test is performed locally to establish a baseline and identify performance bottlenecks. A machine with 1.7 GHz Intel Core i7 processor, 8 GB 1600 MHz DDR3 memory, and OS X Yosemite version 10.10.5 is used to execute the implemented algorithms.

We measure processing time of each function for both data aggregation and data processing modules. Please note that integration of the algorithms which are responsible for extracting malicious activities from darknet data is currently work in progress. Thus, such processing time for such algorithms is not included in the

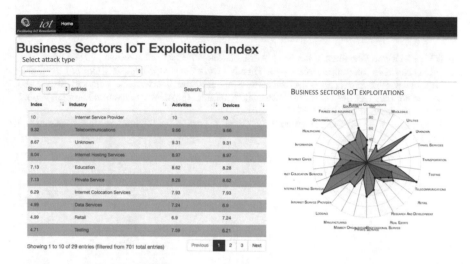

Fig. 4.6 A screenshot of business sectors exploitation index dashboard

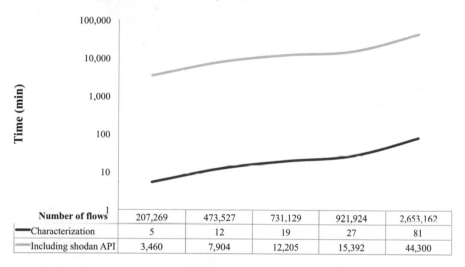

Number of flows	207,269	473,527	731,129	921,924	2,653,162
Characterization	5	12	19	27	81
Including shodan API	3,460	7,904	12,205	15,392	44,300

Fig. 4.7 Elapsed time related to the inference and characterization of unsolicited IoT devices

performance evaluation. It is worthy to pinpoint that all Shodan API methods are rate-limited to 1 request/second. In this context, the inference of IoT devices requires the largest processing time, as illustrated in Fig. 4.7, which demonstrates the elapsed time for performing inference and characterization of IoT unsolicited activities.

Several optimization steps have been identified based on the performed tests, including (1) reducing rate-limitation associated with Shodan API, and (2) parallelization of server-side processes. We are currently exploring these methods.

References

1. D3 Data-Driven Documents. [Online]. Available: https://d3js.org/. Accessed 2018-03-05.
2. UCSD Network Telescope – Near-Real-Time Network Telescope Dataset. [Online]. Available: http://www.caida.org/data/passive/telescope-near-real-time_dataset.xml. Accessed 2018-03-05.
3. MaxMind, Inc. GeoIP2 Databases. [Online]. Available: https://www.maxmind.com/en/geoip2-databases. Accessed 2018-03-05.
4. Shodan®.   Rest API documentation.   [Online]. Available: https://developer.shodan.io/api. Accessed 2018-03-05.

Chapter 5
Concluding Remarks and Future Perspective

The IoT paradigm refers to scenarios where network connectivity and computing capability extends to embedded sensors, allowing these devices to generate, exchange and consume data with minimal human intervention [1]. Such paradigm is being realized and facilitated by critical advancements in computing power, electronics miniaturization, and network interconnections. Indeed, the large-scale deployment of IoT devices promises to transform many aspects of our contemporary lives, offering more personal security, helping to minimize energy consumption, providing the possibility to remodel agriculture, and energy production, to name a few. While IoT deployments have been receiving much hype, their unique characteristics coupled with their interconnected nature indeed present new security challenges. Various technical difficulties, such as limited storage, power, and computational capabilities hinder addressing IoT security requirements, enabling a myriad of vulnerable IoT devices to reside in the Internet-space. Indeed, unnecessarily open ports, weak programming practices coupled with improper software update capabilities serve as entry points for attackers by allowing malicious reprogramming of the devices, causing their malfunction and abuse. Moreover, the insufficiency of IoT access controls and audit mechanisms enable attackers to generate IoT-centric malicious activities in a highly stealthy manner.

In this book, we first shed the light on current research directions and their technical details from a multidimensional perspective focusing on IoT vulnerabilities. We then achieved our primary goal of addressing the imperative tasks of quantifying, characterizing and attributing exploited IoT devices by leveraging the results of active measurements through Internet-wide scanning in conjunction with passive measurements in the context of darknet traffic analysis to shed the light on such devices and analyze their unsolicited network traffic characteristics.

This book indeed presents a solid foundation, in which future research efforts, in this imperative IoT empirical security research area, are currently being planned and pursued. Foremost, a large-scale, more thorough, empirical characterization ought to be conducted to deeply comprehend the severity and magnitude of

© Springer Nature Switzerland AG 2020
E. Bou-Harb, N. Neshenko, *Cyber Threat Intelligence for the Internet of Things*,
https://doi.org/10.1007/978-3-030-45858-4_5

Internet-wide IoT maliciousness. Additionally, the further empirical analysis will be executed to understand the nature of the generated traffic of such compromised IoT devices. Data analytics rooted in the machine and deep learning is also planned to be explored, to provide better characterization and usage of the generated IoT malicious signatures. From an operational cyber security perspective, we continue our work on developing and operating the proposed methodologies in real-time to index and share the obtained insights with the research and security communities at large, to strongly support and facilitate IoT security research using empirical data and aid in the IoT remediation objective at scale.

Besides our future work, we pinpoint that research efforts are also required in the context of studying IoT-specific attacks and their malicious signatures. Indeed, such knowledge is essential in providing effective remediation solutions. Further, suitable schemes, which take into account IoT-specific threats coupled with their unique characteristics, undoubtedly require to be designed and integrated into firmware development cycles to contribute to securing IoT devices.

5.1   Challenges and Future Perspective

In this section, we outline a number of research and operational challenges and pinpoint several initiatives (both technical and non-technical) for future work, which we believe are worthy of being pursued in this imperative field of IoT security.

Challenge 1
One of the most significant challenges for future work is the design and implementation of Internet-scale solutions for addressing the IoT security problem. The widespread deployment of IoT in different private environments prevents visibility of IoT-related security incidents and thus hinders the adequate analysis of such data in order to identify, attribute and mitigate maliciousness. The investigation of empirical data, which enables Internet-scale detection of IoT maliciousness is of paramount importance. A significant hurdle to such approaches involves the development of mechanisms to acquire relevant data in a timely fashion. By building such (operational) capabilities based on empirical measurements, we gain substantial benefits. The first being that such an analysis is non intrusive, thus does not require resources from the IoT network or the devices. The second is related to the collection of sufficient information for generating IoT-centric malicious signatures, which is currently unavailable. These signatures could be deployed at local IoT realms for proactive mitigation.

Possible Future Initiatives
The cyber security capability which leverages Internet-scale empirical measurements and data-driven approaches and methodologies to identify

(continued)

exploited IoT devices would indeed effectively complement currently available approaches to provide IoT resiliency.

There is a paramount need for collaborative knowledge and information exchange regarding the notion of maliciousness from various sources (including ISPs, IoT operations, researchers, etc.) to successfully address the IoT security issue.

Challenge 2

As noted, empirical measurements for inferring IoT maliciousness is essential, yet solely insufficient to secure the IoT paradigm. Indeed, vulnerable yet unexploited IoT devices can not be addresses by employing the latter approach. Consequently, numerous devices remain vulnerable for future exploitation. Although novel ways for vulnerabilities' identification efficiently address a number of IoT weaknesses, they mainly focus on particular devices. Hence, such methods lack device variability and scalability. In this context, there is a need for IoT-tailored testbeds which would enable automated vulnerability assessments for various devices in different deployment contexts.

Possible Future Initiatives

Applying transfer learning algorithms [2] to the currently available knowledge related to IoT vulnerabilities could ameliorate and automate the tasks of vulnerability assessment and simulation in order to extrapolate this knowledge to various IoT devices, platforms and realms. This holds promise to conduct vulnerability assessment in a large-scale to contribute to prompt IoT remediation.

Additionally, investigating innovative IoT-specific trust models [3] that are employed in various contexts would enable the development of proper IoT remediation strategies.

Challenge 3

This challenge addresses secure access to IoT devices and their data. It is indisputable that the ability to gain access to IoT devices by either brute-forcing their default credentials or by exploiting certain vulnerabilities remains a primary attack vector. While modifying default credentials is a necessary strategy, a myriad of legacy IoT devices with hard-coded or default credentials remain in use rendering it possible for an attacker to take advantage of such vulnerabilities to execute various misdemeanors. We noticed that approaches which attempt to address this issue are rarely investigated in the literature. Further, while using traditional password-based access methods are the most frequently employed, new techniques rooted in biometric and context-aware methods are currently emerging for the IoT. However, we noticed the lack of comprehensive analysis, which enables the thorough comprehension of the advantages and disadvantages of these methods along with their corresponding implementation technicalities and challenges.

Possible Future Initiatives

There is need to explore techniques and methods to increase users' awareness about the consequences of potential IoT threats and possible technical and non-technical strategies to reduce the risk of exposure.

Further, developing numerous approaches to enforce credential updates and automate the deployment of frequent firmware updates seems to need much attention from the research community. Such approaches should arise from inferred vulnerabilities using research methodologies (including IoT-malware instrumentation) as well as from IoT industrial (manufacturing) partners and market collaborators.

In addition, a comprehensive analysis of biometric and context-aware access methods would provide valuable insights regarding the level of their security, stability, scalability, and implementation details.

Challenge 4

To assure sufficient level of IoT software security, proper and prompt operational actions should be established for the identified vulnerabilities. From the conducted survey, we noticed a noteworthy shortage of research and development methodologies, which address this issue.

Another problem of significant importance is related to secure IoT code. IoT applications rely on tailored software applications, which could characteristically be vulnerable. We also noticed the lack of methods which aim at vetting deployed IoT code.

Although many software assessment techniques are available, case studies similar to [4] report that nearly 50% of organizations that have deployed IoT never assess their applications from the software security perspective.

Possible Future Initiatives

There is need to execute exploratory studies to inspect the time required from the discovery of IoT vulnerabilities to their disclosure to producing patches and subsequently deploying them at the affected IoT devices. Indeed, this would drive and enhance risk management for the IoT paradigm, especially for those IoT devices deployed at critical CPS environments.

Further, the investigation of the dependencies between weak programming practices and vendors, platforms, device types, and deployment environments would enable the selection of more reliable software vendors as well as encourage vendors to produce more secure code.

Along this line of thought, there is need to enforce stringent IoT programming standards and develop automated code tools to vet IoT applications in order to effectively remediate IoT software vulnerabilities, thus further contributing to IoT security and resiliency.

References

1. Luigi Atzori, Antonio Iera, and Giacomo Morabito. From "Smart Objects" to "Social Objects": The Next Evolutionary Step of the Internet of Things. *IEEE Communications Magazine*, 52(1):97–105, 2014.
2. Oscar Day and Taghi M Khoshgoftaar. A survey on heterogeneous transfer learning. *Journal of Big Data*, 4(1):29, 2017.
3. Yunhan Jack Jia, Qi Alfred Chen, Shiqi Wang, Amir Rahmati, Earlence Fernandes, Z Morley Mao, Atul Prakash, and Shanghai JiaoTong Unviersity. Contexiot: Towards providing contextual integrity to appified IoT platforms. In *Proceedings of The Network and Distributed System Security Symposium*, 2017.
4. Ponemon Institute LLC. 2017 study on mobile and iot application security. [Online]. Available: https://www.arxan.com/wp-content/uploads/2017/01/2017_Security_IoT_Mobile_Study.pdf.

Printed in the United States
by Baker & Taylor Publisher Services